AF607809

ESPERANZA SPEAKS

# ESPERANZA SPEAKS

## Confronting a Century of Global Change in Rural Panama

Gloria Rudolf

TC TEACHING CULTURE

UNIVERSITY OF TORONTO PRESS
Toronto Buffalo London

Toronto Buffalo London
utorontopress.com

ISBN 978-1-4875-9470-1 (cloth)
ISBN 978-1-4875-9469-5 (paper)
ISBN 978-1-4875-9471-8 (EPUB)
ISBN 978-1-4875-9472-5 (PDF)



**Library and Archives Canada Cataloguing in Publication**

Title: Esperanza speaks : confronting a century of global change in rural Panama / Gloria Rudolf.
Names: Rudolf, Gloria, author.
Series: Teaching culture.
Description: Series statement: Teaching culture | Includes bibliographical references and index.
Identifiers: Canadiana (print) 20210139765 | Canadiana (ebook) 20210141441 | ISBN 9781487594695 (softcover) | ISBN 9781487594701 (hardcover) | ISBN 9781487594718 (EPUB) | ISBN 9781487594725 (PDF)
Subjects: LCSH: Loma Bonita (Coclé, Panama) – Economic conditions – 20th century. | LCSH: Loma Bonita (Coclé, Panama) – Social conditions – 20th century. | LCSH: Loma Bonita (Coclé, Panama) – Social life and customs – 20th century. | LCSH: Globalization – Panama – Loma Bonita (Coclé) | LCSH: Ruiz, Esperanza, 1922– | LCSH: Ruiz, Esperanza, 1922 – Family. | LCSH: Loma Bonita (Coclé, Panama) – Biography. | LCGFT: Biographies.
Classification: LCC F1576.L66 R83 2021 | DDC 972.87/21053 – dc23

We welcome comments and suggestions regarding any aspect of our publications – please feel free to contact us at news@utorontopress.com or visit us at utorontopress.com.

Every effort has been made to contact copyright holders; in the event of an error or omission, please notify the publisher.

University of Toronto Press acknowledges the financial assistance to its publishing program of the Canada Council for the Arts and the Ontario Arts Council, an agency of the Government of Ontario.

Canada Council for the Arts
Conseil des Arts du Canada

Funded by the Government of Canada
Financé par le gouvernement du Canada

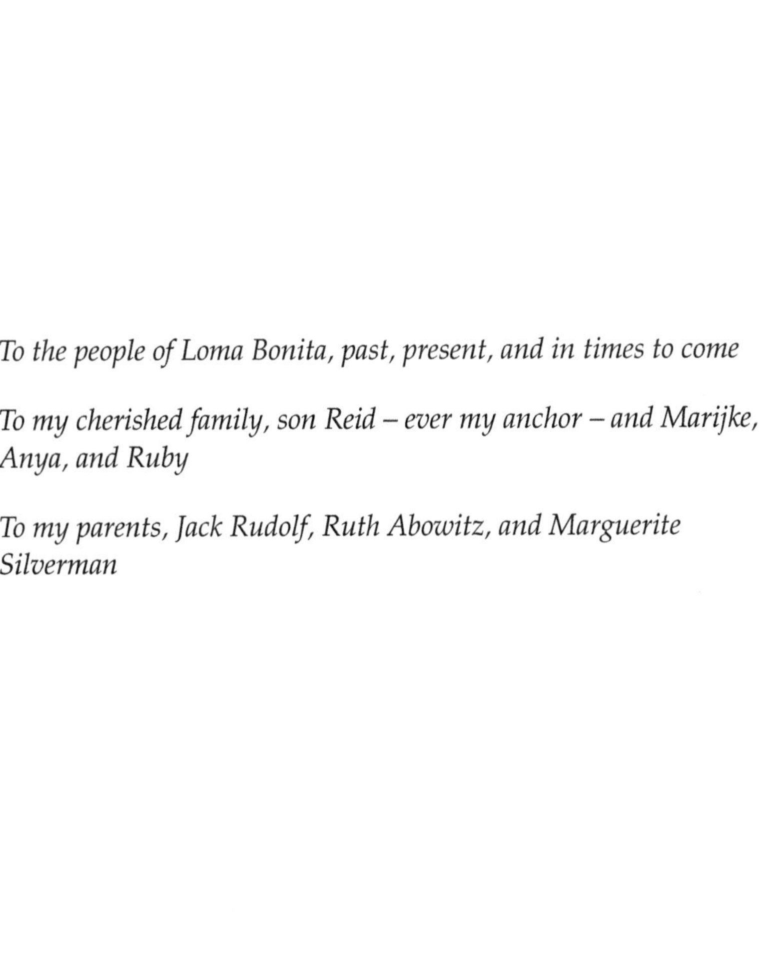

*To the people of Loma Bonita, past, present, and in times to come*

*To my cherished family, son Reid – ever my anchor – and Marijke, Anya, and Ruby*

*To my parents, Jack Rudolf, Ruth Abowitz, and Marguerite Silverman*

*The world will continue, and whether we know it or not, we are deciding its course every day.*

– Gioconda Belli, *The Country under My Skin* (2002)

# Contents

# Illustrations

## Maps



## Figures

# Boxes

# Acknowledgments

Thank you, Esperanza, my teacher, friend, and sometimes-mother, for your half-century gift of trust and tender care across our chasm of difference. Thank you, Andrés, always with me in spirit, and Tony, Viviana, Lety, David, and Sophia for embracing me with open arms and soft hearts throughout the years.

While this book has largely focused on one family in Loma Bonita, every member of this community has welcomed me warmly time and again, taught me about their lives and wishes, and made this work possible. I'm especially grateful to Tina, Francisco, and their six wonderful children for taking a big chance on me 50 years ago, and keeping the door ajar ever since. Tina's contagious laughter and melodic singing are never far from me. I send a special appreciation also to Antonio Ortiz and Narciso Blanco for taking time every field trip to share knowledge and be my guide. To protect the identity but acknowledge the contribution of everyone in Loma Bonita – past and present – I simply list all family surnames: Aguirre, Arcia, Arrocha, Camacho, Castillo, Coronado, Fernández, Franco, García, Gómez, Gonzalez, Guevara, Herrera, Márquez, Martínez, Mora, Morales, Navarro, Ortega, Pérez, Quirós, Rodríguez, Sánchez, Santana, Tenorio, Valdéz.

I could never have carried out my research in Panama all these years without the enormous contributions of my colleague and sister-friend Marcela Camargo Ríos. As past director of the Institute of Historical Patrimony and professor of history at the University of Panama, Marcela helped me navigate authorities and academic life and invited me to share my research in museum and university venues. Giving way beyond professional help, Marcela has honored me with a room of my own in her lovely, plant-filled home where, best of all, I get to hang out with her talented and loving family, including daughter Juana Carlota Cooke Camargo, son-in-law Florencio Díaz Pinzón, and grandson Adrián Despaigne Cooke. Equally important to my work and well-being in Panama has been Marcela's family in Penonomé who for five decades has adopted me as family. I thank first those now gone: grandmother Cornelia Cisneros López, father Réne Camargo Cisneros, and dear mother, Carlota Ríos Sagel. Today, Marcela's sister, Cornelia Camargo Ríos, continues the tradition of beckoning me into her home – with a hug, a meal, a bed, caring conversation, and assistance in finding anything or anyone in Penonomé.

I've had the great fortune of friendship with many colleagues in the capital. Mariela Arce and, until his heartbreaking death, Raúl Leis have played an important role in my political and intellectual education about Panama, not to mention the unforgettable fun we've had together at their home on the magic Island of Taboga. Time and again, I've been the beneficiary of Francisco Herrera's intellectual curiosity, political acumen, and unfailingly empathetic heart. Others who have maintained an interest in my research all these years and kept my spirits buoyed, whenever possible with those Panama beers, include Guillermina De Gracia, Ariel Espino, Carlos Gómez, Beth King, Carlos Guevara-Mann, Eyra Harbar, Luz Graciela Joly, Gisela Lanzas, Belsi Medina, Aixa Quirós, Beatriz Rovira, Alina Torrero, Aimée Urrutia, and Jorge Ventocilla.

This book owes its everything to two of my colleagues and close friends, Hans Buechler and Richard Scaglion. Both have read innumerable drafts of every chapter and given me honest but kindly worded critiques, along with reminders that it was a project worth doing. Hans is a mighty listener, a man who easily gets absorbed into someone's life story. The anthropological analysis is there, but it's the humanity of each person that really draws him in, and that served me well as I struggled to commit Esperanza's life to paper. "It's coming along," he'd say, even when it wasn't, keeping my humanity in mind, too. Richard ("Rich") is a teacher from inside out, one of a few anthropologists of my generation who never tired of teaching "Introduction to Anthropology." This is because he still remembers – and still feels – the excitement of learning about anthropology's "others," people whose ways of living had been unknown, misunderstood, or not even imagined. It was Rich, time and again, who reminded me to keep my focus on those "others" from Loma Bonita, rather than on myself.

Profound thanks go, too, to other colleague-friends and to my son, whose help made this book so much better. Carol Hendrickson, Monica Frölander-Ulf, and Reid R. Frazier commented on a full draft of the book. Carlos Guevara-Mann reviewed one chapter, and Tony Ranere and Richard Cooke read the section on Panama's archaeology and helped with the bibliography. David Brumble shared knowledge and books about narratives of Indigenous North Americans. Mariuxi Cordero and Evan Templeton calmly answered my desperate calls for help with maps and kinship charts, and saw me through computer rebellions.

I want also to acknowledge other friends who have accompanied me on various legs of this book journey: Laurel Bossen, Judie Donaldson, Stephanie Flom, James T.G. Frazier, Beth Goode, Marijke Hecht, Todd Jailer, M. Barbara Leons, Jeff Lesak, Bill Mitchell, Rachel O'Brien, Peter Oresick, Barbara Paull, Joseph Plummer, Cathy Rafael, Joan Ranere, Tony Ranere, Steven Rudolf, Myrna Silverman, Stephanie Studenski, Merrily Swoboda, Cynthia Vanda, Diana Wahle, John Warren, and Mark Weakland.

And, let me not forget to convey my appreciation to three anonymous reviewers who forced me, often reluctantly, to rethink my positions, definitely to the benefit of this book. At the University of Toronto Press, I'm grateful to editors Anne Brackenbury and John Barker for their enthusiasm for this project, and to Carli Hansen for her patience in following it through. Another critical contribution to my work has come from funders, and I send a large measure of gratitude to the Fulbright Program (Fulbright Senior Scholar program [1999–2000] and Fulbright Senior Specialist program [2005]), to the Latin American Council of Social Sciences (CLACSO) and the Center for Latin American Studies (CELA) in Panama (2010), and to the Cultural Office of the US Embassy in Panama (2007 and 2010).

Finally, I owe an everlasting debt to three guardian angels who stayed close by – no matter what: my sister Debbie Manheim, with her weekly "how-are-you-doing" phone calls; sister-friend Karen Miyares, who sent frequent upbeat text messages; and sister-friend Jan Carlino, a fellow gardener, who told me at the beginning, "Remember, you are gardening a book."

# People You Will Meet

**Andrés,** Esperanza's husband. In Loma Bonita, he and Esperanza have lived on land that he inherited from his mother. A farmer all his life, he had five children with Esperanza.

**Belsi,** wife of Esperanza's uncle Dionisio. They had 13 children.

**Benita,** Esperanza's grandmother. As a child, Esperanza loved her and sometimes did agricultural work for her. Benita is married to Natividad.

**Bianca, Felipa, and María,** Esperanza's first cousins and close friends since childhood who assisted her often with urban work and life. They are daughters of Marta and Manuel.

**Cristo,** local political official (*regidor*) in Loma Bonita during the 1970s. He ran as a candidate for office as "Municipal Representative" and was supported by Esperanza and Andrés.

**David,** Esperanza's son. He became a Catholic priest after 16 years of sacrifice, and a great deal of material and emotional support from his parents and siblings.

**Diana,** daughter of one of Esperanza's aunts. As a child, she was brought to Panama City by a teacher, was educated and married there, and helped Esperanza often with urban work and life.

**Dionisio,** Esperanza's uncle. A farmer and cattle raiser all his life, Dionisio and Esperanza's mother, Natalia, had a fight for control of their father's land after their father died. He had 13 children with wife Belsi.

**Esperanza,** one of the first females in Loma Bonita to migrate to the city to work for temporary periods as a live-in domestic. She had five children with husband Andrés.

**Francisco,** host in house where I've lived when in Loma Bonita during the past 50 years. The house is built on land inherited from his father. He taught himself to build cement-block houses and do carpentry, and preferred this to farming. He had six children with wife Tina.

**Janeth,** Esperanza's granddaughter. Child of Viviana, she struggled as a single parent to attend university with help from her mother and siblings.

**José,** husband of Esperanza's daughter Sophia. A construction worker, he helped build the cement-block house of Esperanza and Andrés in Loma Bonita. He has four children with Sophia.

**Lety,** Esperanza's daughter. She left at age 13 to work as a domestic in an urban area. After a long struggle in Panama City, she graduated from sewing school and then worked in a small clothing factory and also independently from her home. Later, she started a food business with her husband in a lowland town. She has two children.

**Manuel,** Esperanza's biological father who is married to Marta, Esperanza's aunt. When Esperanza was born, he gifted Esperanza's mother, Natalia, and her husband, Teodoro, a plot of land in Loma Bonita on which to live and grow food crops. He had 10 children with Marta.

**Marcela,** Esperanza's first cousin. When Marcela had problems with the man she was living with in the city, Esperanza helped her get back to Loma Bonita.

**Marta,** Esperanza's aunt. Her house in Loma Bonita was near the house where Esperanza grew up, and there was a constant exchange of resources and labor between the two families. She had 10 children with husband Manuel.

**Narciso,** Andrés's nephew in Loma Bonita, who has always helped them out with labor and company.

**Natalia,** Esperanza's mother. Esperanza was her first child and lived with her mother for a few years after marrying.

**Natividad,** grandson of Reina Ruiz and Esperanza's grandfather. He raised cattle and farmed in Loma Bonita and was one of the first to grow coffee for sale in the market. Esperanza was born in his house. He is married to Benita.

**Nella,** neighbor in Loma Bonita who was hired to care for Esperanza and Andrés.

**Noris,** Esperanza's daughter-in-law, mother of five children. She had her own cooked-food business in Panama City for years, and sometimes paid her sisters-in-law to work with her.

**Reina Ruiz,** an original settler in Loma Bonita in the 1830s or 1840s.

**Sophia,** Esperanza's youngest child. Sophia left for Panama City at age 15 to work as a domestic and later moved near to Colón with her husband, but has returned often to Loma Bonita to take care of her aging parents. She has four children with husband José.

**Teodoro,** Esperanza's stepfather.

**Tina,** host in house where I've lived when in Loma Bonita during the past 50 years. As a young teenager, she was sent to work as a domestic in urban Panama and continued to migrate back and forth for most of her life. She and Esperanza live near one another and are good friends who exchange food, company, and support. She had six children with husband Francisco.

**Tony,** Esperanza's oldest child. He left for the city at age 18 and stayed as a construction worker. He has five children with wife Noris.

**Viviana,** Esperanza's oldest daughter. She left at age 13 to work as a domestic in an urban area, staying in Panama City, but she has returned often to Loma Bonita to take care of her aging parents. She has four children: Isabel, Sebastián, Alexander, and Janeth.

# The Ruiz Family: Kinship Chart

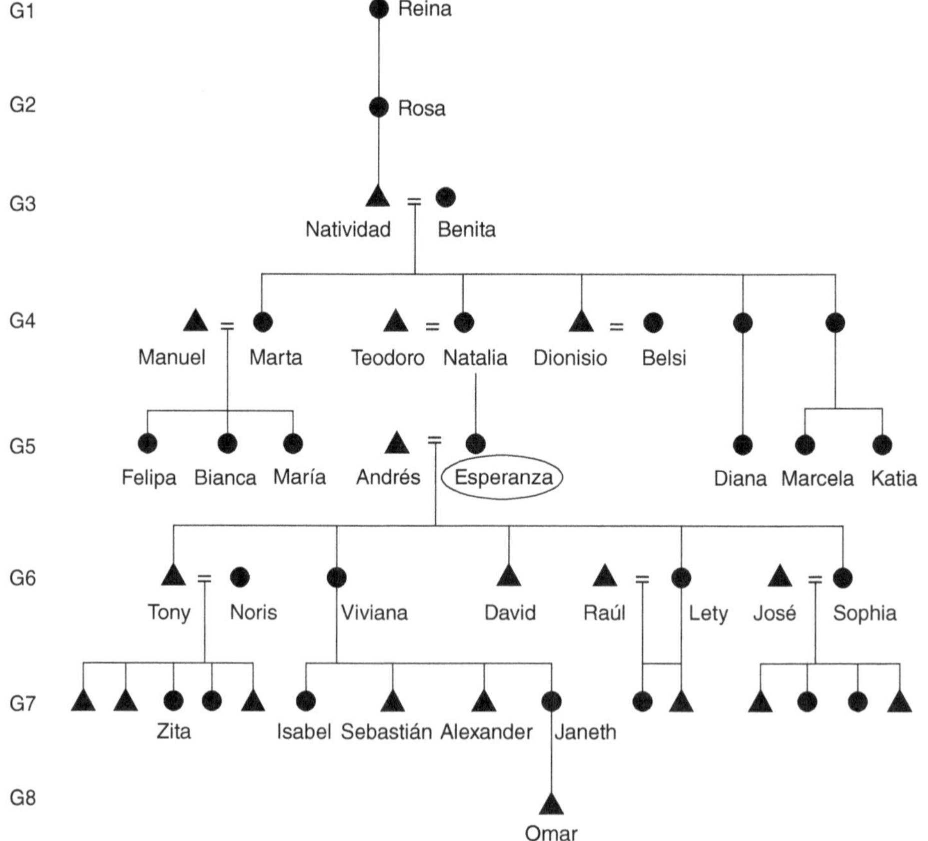

**Map 1. Panama, Bridge of the Americas**

**Map 2. Republic of Panama, Coclé Province**

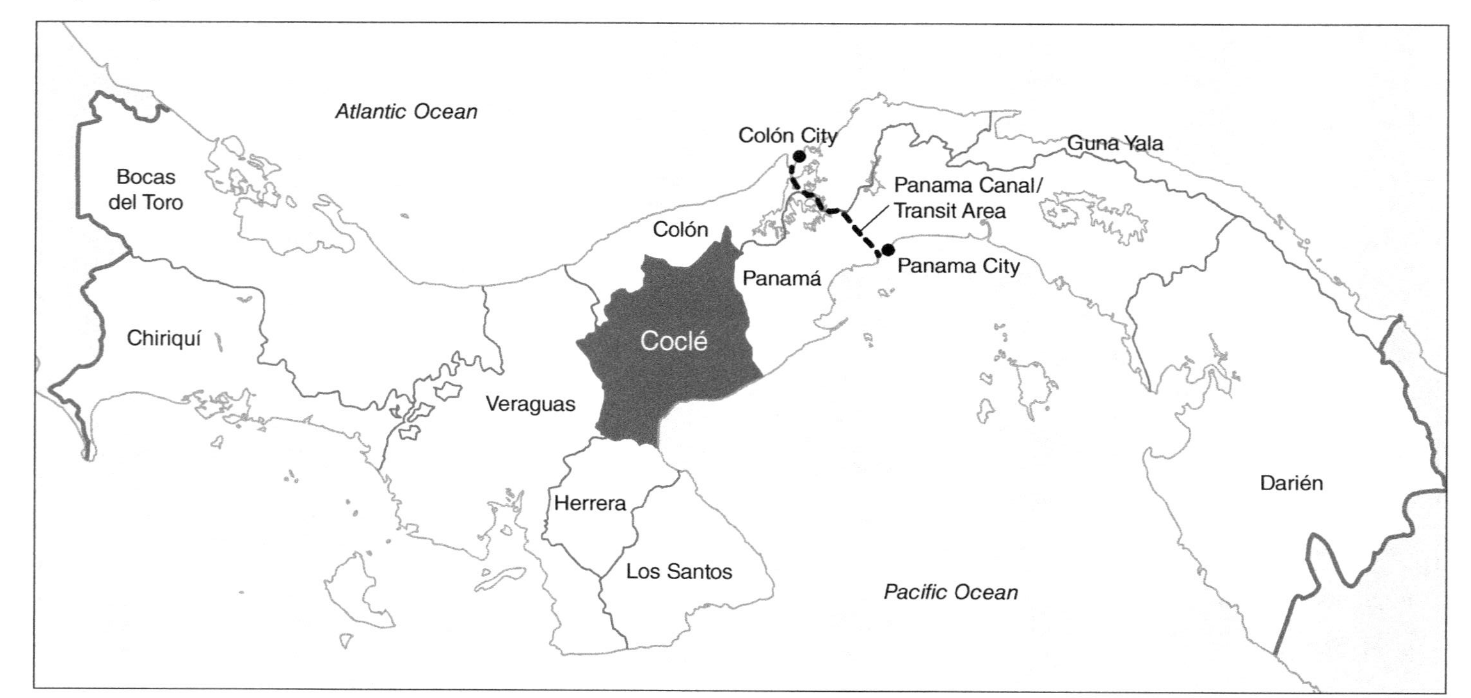

**Map 3. Coclé, El Copé, Loma Bonita, and Frailecito**

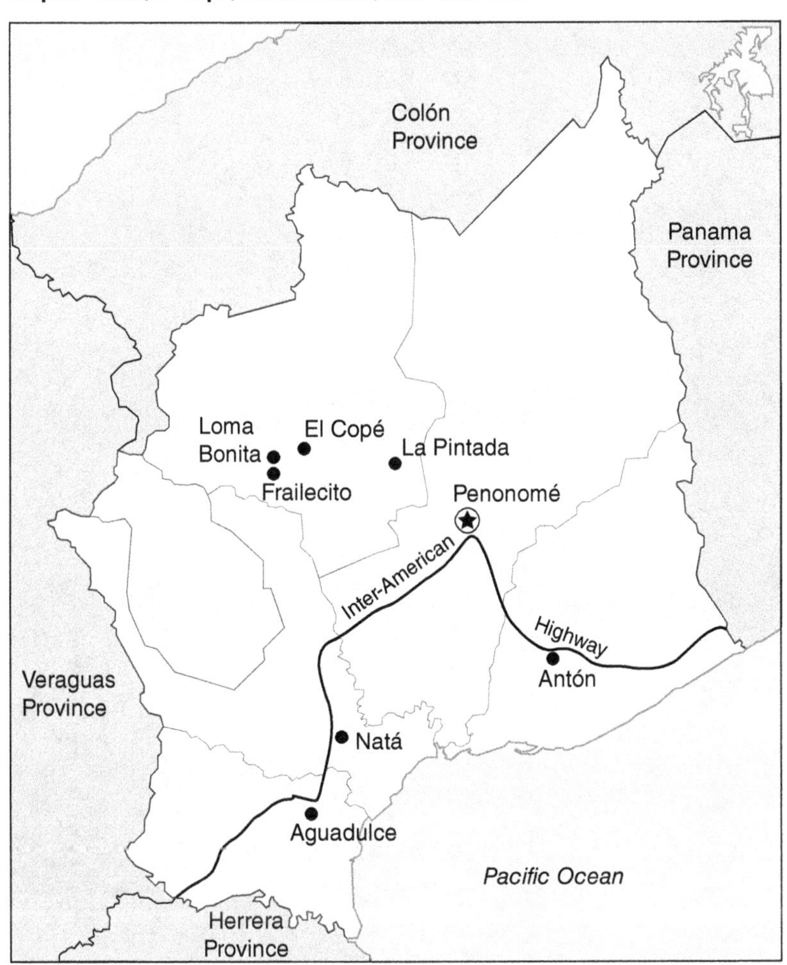

# Introductions

## MY ARRIVAL IN LOMA BONITA, JANUARY 1972*

The door to the white minibus slams shut behind me. Thud! The bus driver throws my three large duffel bags from the car's roof onto the unpaved street, and then jumps down to deliver my two five-gallon jugs of water. Here I am, with much of my year's worth of supplies at my feet, standing along the side of the main street of El Copé, a small community in the mountains of Coclé Province in central Panama (see Maps 1, 2, and 3). Since this is where the paved road ends, the minibus turns around to begin the trip back down the steep, recently paved mountain road. Not another car is in sight. As the sound of the engine fades into the distance, I feel as though the connection to everything I know has been severed. To calm my nerves, I do what I used to do in those days: reach into my forest green canvas shoulder bag for a cigarette, light up, and take a long, deep drag.

That's when I notice that I'm not really alone. Lining the three-block dirt road that is Copé's principal street, I count about 20 small adobe or

* To protect people's identities, I've changed some details and all names in this book, except the surnames mentioned in the book's acknowledgments and the names of historical and contemporary public figures. Esperanza's family members, and most other community members mentioned in more than one scene (and still alive in 2019), have chosen their own pseudonyms. Place names have not been changed.

cement-block houses – and a church, police station, and general store named *La Victoria*. A handful of men in straw hats stand around outside the store, and every one of them is staring at me. Feeling unbearably conspicuous in my white skin, blonde hair, jeans, and sleeveless T-shirt, I force a smile and a greeting. "*Buenos días*" (Good morning), I shout, thoroughly embarrassed to hear my ***gringa*** (US) accent resound throughout the very quiet street.

It's 8:50 a.m. according to the little alarm clock that I pull out of my shoulder bag. Ten more minutes until Señor Ricardo Ortiz is supposed to meet me here with two horses – one for my bags and one for me. This is how I'm to make my way up the mountain to my destination – the even smaller community of Loma Bonita. Mount a horse or climb by foot; these are the only ways to get there during the eight-month rainy season, which just ended.

The arrangement with Sr. Ricardo was made last Saturday, January 8, when I visited Loma Bonita for the first time. I was accompanied then by a student from the University of Panama named Julián, who was interested in my work and could help me with my shaky Spanish. What a momentous day that had been for me! After five long years of studying anthropology and planning for my doctoral research, as well as five weeks here in Panama of looking for the right place to carry it out, I had finally landed in Loma Bonita and quickly felt that this place could work. First, there was the apparent friendliness of the people. During our three-hour climb by foot from Copé to Loma Bonita, Julián and I had been passed by a steady stream of barefooted men and women carrying heavy sacks of coffee down the mountain on their backs. Despite their burdens, almost all took the time to respond to our greeting. The fact that women as well as men were doing the hard physical labor of carrying their coffee to market in Copé was another draw for me, given my interest in studying gender roles.

And, then, there was the beauty of this area. True, I had had a hard time noticing this during that first arduous climb up the mountainside in 90-degree weather. As a non-exercising smoker who had never climbed a mountain in her life, I had my eyes plastered to the ground the entire journey so as not to trip over stones or snakes, or fall while leaping from rock to rock across streams. In fact, it had been all I could do to look up, smile, and greet every person who passed us by. But when we finally reached the first house in Loma Bonita – a small dwelling with adobe walls and a red tile roof – I got a moment to relax and notice the

**Figure I.1. Loma Bonita, houses widely scattered, 2007.**

landscape around me. A barefooted woman stood outside, wearing a stained tan skirt and blouse and a rather tattered straw hat. "*Buenas tardes*" (Good afternoon), she said, her voice so soft-spoken that I had to strain to hear her. She smiled and extended her hand slightly. I reached out to shake it, but she moved it away quickly. Julián and I smiled back, and she invited us onto her patio to rest for a while. Exhausted, soaked in sweat, and thirsty from the long climb up, we eagerly accepted the invitation as well as the cup of coffee she offered. I admit to having had mild trepidation about what this cup would include, but Señora Blanca delivered a delicious steaming brew of dark roasted coffee sweetened abundantly with sugarcane syrup. Sitting there on her low wooden bench sipping that heavenly coffee, I focused at last on the panorama before me. As far as my eye could see were rugged mountain peaks and vertical, forested slopes and valleys set against a light blue sky the color of forget-me-nots. Scattered widely here and there, house rooftops peeked out above the canopy (see Figure I.1). Snaking up, down, and around these sharp slopes was a continuation of the red-brown dirt road we had taken from Copé. This breathtaking scene clinched the deal for me. Yes, I decided with great relief, I want to do my research here.

I had already gotten permission to do my study from the proper government institution in Panama City, but to stay in Loma Bonita I also needed the blessing of the local political official, called the ***regidor***. I asked Sra. Blanca where the *regidor* lived. "Don't worry," she said, "Señor Cristo Soto lives near here, and my daughter, Ramona, can take you there." When called, 12-year-old Ramona emerged from the house, barefooted and ready to be our guide. But Sra. Blanca's idea of "near," didn't match mine. For almost an hour, we climbed slowly down, down, down into a valley on the same red-brown dirt road, sometimes having to maneuver over or around large boulders. Painful blisters formed on my toes as they pushed against my snug sneakers. For most of this trip, we saw no houses, although occasionally I could hear dogs barking and chickens clucking nearby.

Finally, we turned into a narrow dirt path lined by rocks and boulders and leading through a dense stand of coffee and orange trees. The first house I noticed by the side of the path had the now-familiar adobe walls and red tile roof (see Figure I.2), but there was no one in sight. A few minutes later, in a clearing across a small stream, we saw a two-room, picturesque house set in the midst of a riot of trees and bushes – coffee, orange, banana, papaya, mango, coconut, and brilliant red bougainvillea. It was the only cement-block house I'd so far seen here, with a wall partially painted aqua blue. Hens were shuffling around, but I saw no people. "We're almost there," Ramona said, aware that my energy was waning. Right before arriving at Sr. Cristo's house, we passed another clearing in the coffee trees where a man, a woman, and three children were building a house of wood, earth, and straw. Ramona shouted a greeting, and the woman came bounding toward us. Quite heavy set and wearing a bright kelly-green dress, she moved faster than I would have guessed she could manage with so much weight. "Where are you going," she asked, looking me directly in the eyes in a way that no one from here had done before. She seemed to be middle-aged, and was a head shorter than my own 5 feet 2 inches. Below her torn straw hat, two black braids reached almost to her waist. "We're going to talk with Sr. Cristo Soto, the *regidor*," I answered. "Welcome to Loma Bonita. My name is Esperanza Ruiz," she said, smiling so broadly that I could see she had no front teeth. "Thank you. My name is Gloria, and this is my friend, Julián. *Mucho gusto*" (I'm glad to meet you), I responded, returning the smile.

**Figure I.2. Adobe house with red tile roof, 1972.**

Within minutes of taking leave from Sra. Esperanza, we arrived at the home of the *regidor*. There was a moment of terror when two growling dogs came speeding at us, but Sr. Cristo emerged from the house in time to stop the impending carnage. Like everyone I had met so far, he was not much taller than me. He approached barefooted and donning a well-worn straw hat. What struck me immediately was his ultra-serious-looking face, with pitch black eyes set against very light brown skin. We exchanged greetings and introductions, a task at which Julián excelled, and then I told Sr. Cristo about my mission. "I'm a university student from the United States, and would like to come live here for about a year to learn what life is like in Loma Bonita." His serious-looking face turned incredulous. After all, I later would learn, few lowlanders ever came up to Loma Bonita even briefly, let alone for a yearlong stay. Women. No. A white woman from another country. Never.

Sr. Cristo hesitated, and Julián saved the day. "She has permission papers from the government office sponsoring studies like this in Panama," he said. That did it. From then on, Sr. Cristo couldn't have been more accommodating. "OK," he decided, "you can live at the school in the teachers' house." I had expected this suggestion but wanted instead to live with a family so as to have a better chance of becoming part of the community. So I tried negotiation. "Since I'm alone, with my family far away, Sr. Cristo, I'm hoping to be able to live with a family." After a moment of reflection, he responded. "Well, you might be comfortable living with Dionisio Ruiz's family." I had done some homework before coming to Loma Bonita and had learned that Dionisio Ruiz was the "richest" person in this community. I knew I didn't want to live there either since that could limit my relationships with everybody else. Suddenly visions of that picturesque house nearby danced in my head. I said, "Right before getting to your house, Sr. Cristo, we passed a cement-block house that looked comfortable. Could I stay with that family?" Without delay, Sr. Cristo sent a young girl to fetch the man of that family, and five minutes later, Francisco Soto joined us. Said Sr. Cristo to Francisco, "This woman is a university student from the United States who wants to learn about life here in Loma Bonita and live with your family. Is that OK?" With me standing right there, what could poor Francisco Soto say but yes? I thanked him profusely and said that I'd be back with my things in a week. Sr. Cristo promised that a man named Ricardo Ortiz would meet me in Copé with two horses at 9 a.m. the following Sunday, January 16.

~

That's today, January 16! It's now 9:10 in the morning, but no Sr. Ricardo has appeared. Has he forgotten?

I'm standing by the side of Copé's unpaved main street in exactly the same spot where the minibus had left me. With so many heavy belongings at my feet, I can't go anywhere. There's no place to sit, so I shift from foot to foot, and light up one cigarette after another. About a dozen adults and some kids have now congregated in the street near me, staring and wordless. I periodically smile and say hello, and a giggle or a greeting is sometimes returned. But no one has dared come over to talk with me. In addition to feeling alone and conspicuous, I'm sweating profusely under my thick jeans – Panama's powerful sun is already ablaze. And, where there's sweat in Panama, mosquitoes buzz. They're headed right for my bared arms, neck, and ankles.

It's 9:30 a.m., and still no Sr. Ricardo. Then, 10 a.m. Just when despair makes its appearance, so does Sr. Cristo Soto, Loma Bonita's *regidor*. The sight of this man brings involuntary tears of relief trickling down my cheeks. "*Buenos días*" (Good morning), we greet one another. He explains that Sr. Ricardo had gone to a saint's day festival in the lowlands yesterday and had not been able to get a car back to Copé to meet me this morning. Instead, he, Cristo, has come to help, but alas, without a horse. He suggests that I leave my bags with a nearby family and climb up with him by foot to Loma Bonita, promising to send a horse down for my things later. My chest tightens with anxiety. How can I leave all these material possessions that I'll need in my new life to an entirely unknown fate? Yet the only alternative is to turn around and go home, which is not really an option. So I let go of my need to control my things and my destiny for now. I say, "*Vamos,* Sr. Cristo." (Let's go.)

After dropping off my bags, we walk the three blocks or so to the very steep, red-brown dirt road that winds its way up to Loma Bonita and beyond. I tell Sr. Cristo how embarrassed I am about my lack of climbing skills and how difficult a time I had had last week getting there on foot. He tells me not to worry. "We'll walk slowly," he says. Ha! I have trouble keeping up with his "slow" pace, despite the fact that, in his late fifties, he has three decades on me. We have to stop twice in the first half hour so I can catch my breath. But then, like magic he appears. Sr. Ricardo's teenaged son, Carlos, meets us on his way down the mountain to Copé to rescue me. And Carlos has a horse!

Carlos and Sr. Cristo hold the small brown horse in place while I eagerly climb into a most uncomfortable saddle. I decide not to mention that I've never mounted a horse before in my life. I'm not overly afraid, though, because one of them holds the reins and guides the horse the whole time. I can now relax and pay attention to the landscape, sounds, and rhythms all around me. A tranquil world surrounds us. Other than our voices and footsteps, there is only the clop, clop, clop of the horse; a myriad of unfamiliar birdcalls; the burbling of stream water; and the occasional, distant squawk of a rooster or clang of a machete hitting a tree.

Up, up we go along the dirt road lined in places by tall trees, low shrubs, and purple wildflowers, and crisscrossed here and there by small streams. Twice we veer off the main road to take a shortcut over, instead of around, a hill, and we see scrawny cattle with protruding ribs grazing freely. Sr. Cristo tightens his grip on the reins of my horse and explains that the cattle occasionally attack people who get in their way. So precipitous are these shortcuts that I'm certain my horse and I are almost parallel to the ground. My thighs and butt are paying a price. Straight up we climb for about an hour until we reach a summit.

"This is Loma Bonita," Sr. Cristo announces, pointing all around. Before me once again stretches the view that last week took my breath away. This time I notice how wonderfully green the landscape is because of the tropical rains that fall in this part of Panama between April and December. I tell Sr. Cristo and Carlos that I can now understand why someone gave this place the name Loma Bonita (Pretty Hill).

From the summit, we begin almost an hour's descent into the part of Loma Bonita where I'll live for the next year. Soon, we cross the stream that runs by the little picturesque house that will be my home. Two scrawny black dogs come rushing toward us barking furiously but are called back by the man and woman standing in the front patio. Francisco Soto, Tina Peña, and their four children, each younger than ten, are waiting for us. Everyone is barefooted and wearing a woven straw hat. Getting off that horse is no small matter, given my bruised lower parts, but I manage. We three approach the family, and introductions begin; I revel in being the tallest person in my new family. When I reach out to clasp Tina's hand in an enthusiastic handshake, she pulls her hand back quickly after only lightly touching mine, just as Sra. Blanca had done last week. I make a mental note that a woman-to-woman handshake is different here. The children, as in Copé, stand silently and stare. Francisco, who walks with a slight limp, hardly makes eye contact or conversation, and soon slips away.

The socializing is left to Tina. She's a talkative woman with a high-pitched voice and a giggle that seems nervous to me. I learn that she's in her midthirties and born and raised in a community a few hours climb further up the mountain from Loma Bonita. She's beautiful: unusually light brown eyes and short curly hair, cinnamon-colored skin, and the first adult I've yet met from Loma Bonita who isn't missing her two front teeth. Her pink cotton dress seems more "modern" and less faded than others I've noticed in this rural world. The minute I find an opening, I call her aside to ask where I can go to pee. She leads me to the back of the house and points to a stand of coffee trees about 50 yards away. I make my way there in search of a spot devoid of biting ant colonies, snakes, or scorpions, and find that I also have to keep shooing off four scraggy-looking dogs that have accompanied me and now wait nearby like vultures.

Back on the patio, I join Sr. Cristo and Carlos sitting on low wooden benches. Francisco, Tina, and the children have disappeared into the house. A couple of neighbors pass by and stop to say hello. The atmosphere around our conversation ranges from uncomfortable to painful. I smile, listen, ask questions about their lives in my halting Spanish, and answer their questions about mine. How long does it take to get to the United States? [*A full day.*] Where do you live? [*Pittsburgh, Pennsylvania, in the northeast part of the country.*] How old are you? [*Thirty.*] Do you have children? [*No.*] Are you married? [*Yes, my husband is working at home.*] How long have you been married? [*Eight years.*] Tina comes out of the house, and we're alone for a moment. Taking advantage of the privacy, she comes up close to me and whispers, "How can you be married for so long but not have any children?" I take a gamble and explain about my diaphragm and its jelly. She's never heard of such a thing, she says, almost doubled up with laughter over the "jelly."

For the rest of this long, long day, I'm anchored to the bench on the patio. Actually, I'm feeling as miserable as I ever remember feeling. My thighs and butt ache from the horse ride. I'm also hot, sweaty, tired, hungry, thirsty, and scared, and I have a nonstop headache from straining to understand and speak Spanish. Maybe the hardest part is that I have to keep smiling, making small talk, appearing to be cheerful, excited, enthusiastic, and energetic with everyone who shows up.

Finally, at about 5 p.m., Tina takes me to the back patio of the house where she has set up a small wooden table and chair under a tree. I sit there all alone, and she serves me a tasty plate of rice and beans with a fried egg and **plantain**, followed by a delicious cup of coffee, equal to the one served by Sra. Blanca last week. After dinner, Tina shows me to my quarters. Separating the rooms in this two-room house is a 10-foot adobe wall that doesn't quite reach the ceiling. She and Francisco sleep in one of the rooms, the other is divided in half by a shorter 7-foot high adobe partition. The four children get to sleep in one bed in one half of the room, and I get the other. At the moment my half is empty save a handmade broom that Tina has left so I can sweep the earth floor.

It isn't until 7 p.m. that Sr. Cristo and Sr. Ricardo arrive with the horse that carries my bags and water. Soon Sr. Cristo's wife shows up to gift me tangerines. She disappears quickly into the kitchen, a separate thatched-roof structure without walls in the back patio of the house, where Tina and the children are congregated. I'm left with the men out front, and conversation shifts to politics. "You're invited to our school meeting on Tuesday," Sr. Cristo tells me. "We'll be planning for a dance to make money for the school. That's when I can introduce you to the community." I accept the invitation, already nervous about what I'll say. Even more worrying is Sr. Cristo's second invitation. "Sergeant Vito Delgado of the National Guard knows you're here and wants to meet you." "With pleasure," I lie.

I know that a few years ago Panama's military, the National Guard, overthrew the country's civilian government and sent armed military men into the countryside to live and, ostensibly, help improve rural people's lives. In fact, my research aims to understand the impacts of this military presence on the social and economic conditions of the women and men of Loma Bonita (Chapter 4). But truthfully, the specter of armed policemen everywhere scares me personally, and I'm sure it will politically complicate my relationships in these mountains.

It's about 8 p.m. and dark when at long last these neighbors stand to leave. Tina rushes over to catch Sr. Cristo's ear and asks him to bring a desk for me from the school. "Yes," he says, "and treat her well, niece." Ah, I make a mental note, they're kin. Francisco disappears somewhere into the shadows. Tina grabs her kerosene lantern and leaves to put her four children to bed; I hear her teaching them a Catholic prayer. I'm alone for the first time since arriving in Copé. The night air is cool, but not cold. The stars and half-moon feel near enough to touch. I pull my flashlight from my canvas bag and walk toward the coffee trees to pee. Oh no! The battery goes dead, and there's no light in this world without electricity to look for batteries in my duffel bags. The nearest tree must suffice. I can only pray that no one sees me.

I'm unspeakably tired and ache all over. But I remind myself of this: I made it. I'm here. I've got my canvas cot and sleeping bag set up, and half a room designated as my space. The people have been kind and way more talkative than I dreamed possible. My Spanish … well, it sufficed. And the food isn't scary at all. I can do this. I know I can!

## MEETING ESPERANZA AND HER FAMILY

I've been here for only two weeks and am already facing a crisis. It started yesterday morning when Tina called me to breakfast. Like every day since my arrival, I'd walked to the open area in the back of the house where the solitary wooden table and chair awaited me under the tree. Like every other day, the food looked enticing, but eating it all alone felt sad. I'd twice mentioned my desire to eat with the whole family, but Tina hadn't responded; we'd not yet found any comfort zone between us. Yesterday, though, I knew something was different because, instead of giving the usual nervous giggle and immediately exiting after delivering my meal, Tina had lingered near the table. Finally, the words tumbled out. "I want to tell you that tomorrow I'm leaving to work for a while in Panama City – while the kids are on school vacation." She explained that her sister had come by last week to tell her that the nuns at the Catholic high school where she was working had requested that Tina come cook and clean for them.

> They'll pay me $30 a month, and give me a room, and food and clothes and stuff for the house. See that great big pot over there in the corner of the kitchen? They gave it to me last time I worked there.

Sounding apologetic, Tina mentioned that she and Francisco needed money to buy food and pay for school uniforms and notebooks. "Francisco doesn't have much construction work right now; in Loma Bonita there's no money to pay him," she said.

The whole time she was talking, I was thinking, "But, what about me?" Instead I said, "I'm glad you found the work you need, Tina. Who will take care of the children while you're gone?" Francisco and his family and her mother would also help out, she told me. I wanted to scream, "What about me?" but I waited, more accustomed by now to the slow and indirect way that people communicate in Loma Bonita. A few seconds later – which seemed like forever – she added, "You can still live here with us. But Francisco isn't much of a cook, so I've talked with Aunt Esperanza and she has agreed to cook for you."

Relief. Esperanza's house was just a five-minute walk away, and she had seemed friendly when I met her my first day in Loma Bonita. The same went for her husband, Andrés, who had stopped by here yesterday on his way to Copé and offered to take a letter I had written to Copé's post office. "I'll miss you, Tina," I said. "Thank you for your wonderful hospitality and cooking." I wondered whether she was really leaving, in part, to escape the hard work and *pena* (embarrassment) of taking care of me. Acute *pena* still accompanies me everywhere, with everyone, every day in Loma Bonita.

~

Now, as I approach the front patio of Esperanza and Andrés's house for my first dinner with them, my heart is in a knot, my stomach queasy, like right before a "blind date." "*Oiy, Oiy,*" I yell out, having adopted one of the region's high-pitched greeting calls that sound something like tropical bird-speak. "*Oiy, Oiy,*" Esperanza mimics back as she comes running to greet me and call off Capitán, the dog, before he can attack. Like the first time I saw her, I'm struck by the speed with which her plump body moves through space.

She is followed by Andrés who welcomes me too. Andrés Blanco is a skinny man with a contagious smile and eyes so dark that the skin around them has a blackish tinge. The patio is topsy-turvy. Under construction are two one-room structures – a house and a kitchen – both made of wood posts and thatched walls and roofs. Tina had mentioned that Esperanza and Andrés live most of the year in **Frailecito**, a community a couple of hours walk away, but come to Loma Bonita to harvest their coffee during the dry season from January to April. This house site in Loma Bonita is where Andrés grew up, on land that his grandfather gave to his mother.

The kitchen is so small that the waist-high woodstove consumes most of its space, leaving little room for human traffic, let alone anything like a dining table for the family (see Figure I.3). And so, strewn around outside the kitchen are low wooden benches and logs that offer seating. Three of Esperanza and Andrés's children are in this kitchen area when I arrive. The oldest son, 17-year-old Tony, is standing at the woodstove cooking something. Sitting nearby on a log are 11-year-old David, who smiles sweetly, and 8-year-old Sophia, whose thick black braids reach down to her waist. They all think it fun to mimic my greeting. "*Oiy, Oiy,*" each calls out, clearly amused. Esperanza invites me to sit on one of the low wooden benches.

**Figure I.3. Esperanza and Andrés in front of their kitchen, 1970s.**

Soon, everyone takes a seat near me. My heart sings; finally, I won't have to eat alone. Esperanza serves us each a metal soup plate loaded with rice and beans. Sitting in the middle of this construction site, plates in laps, we talk. The conversation is relaxed. I ask them questions. What are their plans for tomorrow? Esperanza will harvest coffee with her brother. Andrés will stay home to continue building the kitchen. David and Sophia, on school vacation, will help their father, and Tony will join his uncle's ***junta*** (a cooperative labor group) to cut down trees and bushes on a plot of his uncle's land. They throw me some questions too. "Where did you go today?" asks Esperanza. My response is honest, but measured, since I need to figure out how to keep my interactions with everyone in this small community of three-dozen households totally confidential. "Today I visited all the houses up there in Caña Blanca," is all I say. Before long, jokes and laughter take center stage. I contribute. "I made a mistake today," I say, struggling to suppress a smile. "Someone asked if I was hungry. Instead of saying, *Sí tengo hambre* [Yes, I'm hungry], I said, *Sí, tengo hombre* [Yes, I have a man]!" Everyone joins in the hilarity.

The mood is perfect, and I give my planned speech about how I hope to join them for two meals a day and be given the same food as everyone else, nothing special. Esperanza says, "Sure, Gloria." Everyone

**Figure I.4. Esperanza washing clothes at stream, 1972.**

smiles in agreement. Who knows what they're really thinking, but I've said my piece.

Dinner is done, and Esperanza and Andrés collect dirty plates and walk over to the two big boulders at the edge of the patio. I follow. "Can I help?" I ask. "No need for you to do that, Gloria," says Esperanza. "But I'd love to help you," I insist. "In my house at home, whoever doesn't cook gets to wash dishes." "OK," she says. "Here's how we do it."

Esperanza empties the few leftovers into a large half-gourd for the animals. Then she cleans our plates, spoons, and gourd cups in a plastic basin with lightly soaped-up water and hands them to me. I dip a clean, large half-gourd into another basin filled with clear water from the stream and rinse off the soap. (Esperanza washes clothes in the same stream; see Figure I.4.) Then I stack everything on a nearby rock; later she brings it all into the kitchen area and places it in a big wrought-iron pot covered by a wooden tray that helps protect things from the army of cockroaches and other critters that descend in the night.

While we work, conversation is nonstop. With her protruding lower lip, Esperanza points to the objects of her stories about chickens, thievery, and women's hat weaving in Loma Bonita. She gives me detailed instructions about how to make corn beer and about coffee, explaining that one must roast it only in late afternoon, so as not to get wet afterwards and bring on a terrible fever. She asks me about my husband, and I tell her how Jim supports my university studies. Taking advantage of this moment of relative comfort, I ask how much money I'll owe them for my two daily meals. "I don't know," she says, looking down, embarrassed for the first time. I softly insist, and finally get my answer: 50¢ a day. Phew! Since Tina had been emphatic about not charging me any rent – "No one ever pays to sleep in Loma Bonita," she had said – I'll have enough money to stay for the year. Aside from a small travel grant from my anthropology department back home, my budget rests mainly on the $500 I recently inherited from my uncle Joe.[1]

Nightfall is approaching when I get back to Francisco and Tina's after dinner. Everyone is settling into bed. In my room, I light the kerosene lantern that Tina has lent me until I can buy my own. From my shoulder bag I pull out a small notebook in which I've scribbled "memory notes" to myself all day long. This is my time, my only time, to write my daily fieldnotes. In a larger notebook that I keep in my duffel bag, I write about every detail of my day. Under the topic of "Economics," I include what Esperanza said about chickens and thievery, and in a section on "Gender," I record her information about hat weaving and my observation about how she and Andrés both carried the dirty dinner dishes to the basin for washing. At the end, in a part I call "Personal Research Notes," I write,

> After my first meal with Esperanza and Andrés tonight, I feel exhilarated. I think I've found my first family in Loma Bonita, and, in Esperanza, someone to teach me how to live here, and tell me stories about her life.

I could write all night, but by 10:00 p.m. I can barely see my notebook. It's seething with noisy insects that pass through the glassless windows and head for the only light on this mountainside. Mine. I quit.

## THIS BOOK

### Themes

Esperanza continued to tell me stories about her life throughout my time in Loma Bonita in 1972, and then continued to do so for the next half-century during my 19 subsequent research visits to the community, the most recent one in 2019. As you can imagine, in the course of this half-century, I've witnessed and documented many changes in this place called Loma Bonita.

A hundred years ago, it was a small community of poor but relatively independent **subsistence** farmers. The food crops they planted and the animals they tended met most of their survival needs. Typically, a person was born, raised, married, and buried in or near Loma Bonita. While they sometimes climbed down to the lowlands for religious rituals or small-scale trade negotiations, these were short-term ventures. Lowlanders, for their part, rarely made the strenuous climb up the slopes to visit this highland region. Even more remote for Loma Bonita's residents was the capital, Panama City, a journey that could take a week or more by foot, horse, and/or boat. Today, in contrast, members plant coffee and oranges to sell in the national and global market, and every family, of necessity, has many members who work for wages and live far away in Panama's cities and towns. A person's world has become defined by the back-and-forth movement between rural and urban space of relatives, money, goods, ideas, and services. Travel to the capital is only a half-day trip by car now, and communication between Loma Bonita and the city can be a cell-phone call away. Children and grandchildren living in the city come to spend holidays in the community armed with smart phones and the latest fashion. They talk to each other on Facebook and WhatsApp. In short, today Loma Bonita and the wider global world are directly and routinely linked.

In this book, I trace the path of this century-long transformation that has brought Loma Bonita's people – their production, labor, and land – into the orbit of Panama's national and global capitalist economy. Through the lives of Esperanza Ruiz and her family, I examine how and why this transformation happened, and its impacts on the community. Esperanza is singled out as the central character in this history because I think she'll be as great a teacher for you as she's been for me. Born in 1922, Esperanza has witnessed most of the changes brought by capitalist development in Loma Bonita, and is a keen observer and interpreter of her community's saga. She's an outspoken, warm-hearted woman, and a magnificent storyteller, knowing just when to quicken or slow down the tale she's telling to keep her listener intrigued. In four chapters examining Esperanza's childhood, youth, adulthood, and elder years – and another chapter featuring her children and grandchildren – I share what I've learned from them about family and community and about socioeconomic and cultural change, and I compare their experiences with those of other community families. The broad contours of Loma Bonita's experience are not unique. They've played out not only in a multitude of other rural Panamanian communities but also throughout Latin America and the Global South. To provide a glance at important aspects of this larger picture, I've included separate sections throughout the book titled "A Wider Lens."

The focus in this book on the lived experiences of real people is meant to drive home a major point: that ordinary people have an enormous capacity to face their difficult life conditions head on and to make changes in their lives that sometimes turn out to their own, and others', benefit. On the one hand, Loma Bonita's people have clearly been victims; they've had very few economic or political resources at their disposal to confront novel problems or take advantage of fresh opportunities brought by national and global changes. Over time, their economic position in the face of increasing connection with the capitalist world has left them with more access to goods and services but less in command of their everyday existence, and more dependent for survival on distant markets and political forces over which they have no influence. Yet victimization is only part of their story. As active agents in their own lives, Loma Bonita's residents have drawn creatively on whatever assets and relationships have been at their disposal in pursuit of small advantages to help them survive or surmount their shifting possibilities. Sometimes their choices and actions have led to improvement in their circumstances; sometimes not. This book documents the nature of and reasons for these varied outcomes and digs below the surface to explore how economic and gender inequalities within and between Loma Bonita's families have advantaged some over others in their struggle with the challenges of changing times.

Most often we learn about globalizing capitalism from the top down; powerful government officials and corporate elites dominate the landscape. We lose sight of what "regular" people are doing on the ground, and fail even to ask about the importance of their actions. When, instead, we view change from the bottom up, foregrounding the lives and the humanity of people like Esperanza and her family, it becomes clear that ordinary people can influence how history unfolds.

You'll see that the specific way that global capitalism has developed in Loma Bonita has depended not only on decisions by powerful outsiders but also on how various community members have chosen to act upon the options available to them.

The same global system that reaches into places like Loma Bonita offers the rest of us a range of options for action in our own lives. I hope that what you'll learn in this book from Esperanza and her family will help you make choices that can benefit people like them as well as yourselves. We are all linked as history makers, with a role to play in shaping the future of economic and sociocultural change around the world.

## Fieldwork

### ORIGINAL, 1972

I arrived in Loma Bonita in January 1972 with my major research questions in hand. Guided by theories about worldwide capitalist development in (then-called) Third World countries such as Panama, I wanted to learn what happens when new government programs that aim to alleviate rural poverty enter a community that, like Loma Bonita, had never before received outside public assistance. More specifically, how do these programs affect poorer families versus those better off economically (class), as well as women versus men (gender)?

I learned about such complicated questions by living in Loma Bonita as a "participant observer."[2] This meant that I devoted my days in the community to participating in every aspect of life open to me while at the same time observing all that my eyes and ears could see and hear. Some days, for example, I'd just hang out with Esperanza or another woman, sharing life stories while we washed our clothes at the stream or she prepared food for the next meal. Other days, I'd climb up and down the slopes to visit a family or two that had invited me for conversation or a person who had agreed to a more formal interview – sometimes tape-recorded (in later years, digitally) – about their family genealogy, their thoughts on political or religious matters, or their history of agricultural or wage labor. Alternatively, I'd accompany one or more people to their fields to learn how they planted rice or harvested coffee, or I'd go to Loma Bonita's school to attend a political meeting or a benefit dance, or, if invited, a prayer session at someone's home or a baby's birth. Sometimes, instead, I'd spend a day or more traveling with a community member to visit a relative elsewhere in the highlands or the city.

While my daily activities varied greatly, one thing never did: before going to sleep, I'd write my fieldnotes. From the shoulder bag or backpack that I'd carried around all day, I'd pull out a notebook in which I had jotted down reminders about things to record later. Then, in a larger notebook, I'd write an account of what I did, saw, heard, felt, and learned that day. No detail was too small for my fieldnotes.

This way of learning through participant observation may seem like a simple, straightforward, even fun way to investigate social life, but actually it's a method of doing research that's packed with complexities and problems. In this work, nothing matters more than being able to form relationships of mutual respect and trust. And nothing could be more difficult. Take, as one example, my interest in understanding the nature of class and gender inequalities in Loma Bonita, which, as noted, was central to my proposed research. From the beginning, this meant trying to avoid becoming associated in most people's minds with the richest community members, with men, or with military government officials, because those associations could breed more mistrust about me among everyone else. To meet this challenge, I had to figure out how everyone around me fit into this puzzle and then consciously seek out the company and advice of Loma Bonita's poorer families before richer, women before men, and community members before government officials.

Further complicating these efforts to build good relationships with all of Loma Bonita's people was the reality of my privileged position. I was keenly aware that, in the eyes of each community member, I was not only a stranger but also a white-skinned, middle-class university student from the US, a person who sat way higher up in the global socioeconomic hierarchy than they. To try to mitigate our vast social divide, I worked to "level our playing field," doing things like memorizing community paths so I wouldn't need guides and traveling light so as not to need help carrying things. These efforts on my part were not meant to belie the reality of our inequalities but to give us a chance to form relationships based on our common humanity; fieldwork (like life) is as much a matter of heart as of mind. The best I could do was make an effort to be clear in my mind, and later in my writings, about the nature and implications of our power differences.[3]

While my attempts to humanize our relationships had plenty of ups and downs, they did help me in the course of that first year to build enough mutual trust and respect to become welcomed in most of Loma Bonita's 36 households and to learn from most residents – poorer as well as better off, women as well as men. My deepest relationships and insights, though, were undoubtedly with women.

## RETURNING, AGAIN AND AGAIN

It wasn't until six years later, in 1979, that I was able to return for another field trip. A sweet return. Smiles all around. For the families of Tina and Esperanza, who agreed once again to provide my room and meals, I arrived with gifts of clothing and a small cash offering scaled to the amount of money that a migrant family member might bring home; once again, I was financing this field visit myself and had a tight budget. To all other Loma Bonita families, I offered a *recuerdo* (memento) – a ziplock bag (in itself desirable) containing a pen, pencil, and hair ornament that I delivered door to door. These were precious visits that took almost two weeks to complete, but they gave us time to catch up on news – and to remember trust. And it gave me the chance to display a copy of the dissertation I had written based on my 1972 research in the community and to explain its main points. This was just a gesture, of course, since it was written in English, but one that, at least, partially responded to one woman's question back in 1972: "What do you do with all these words I give you?"

My research agenda during that return visit to Loma Bonita focused on labor migration to Panama's cities and towns, a topic that had turned out to be the focus of my dissertation. I had had to nix my original plan to write about the effects of the government's projects in Loma Bonita in order to avert any chance of political retribution to community members who had been against the military government.

I could not have imagined back then, in 1979, that this return field visit would be followed by 18 others in the course of the next 40 years. Keeping track of people's unfolding lives and the community's unfolding history had become my passion. And my mission? To describe and explain the long-term impacts of capitalist development on ordinary people by revisiting the same people in the same place over many years. It's my view that participant observation fieldwork, despite its complications and limitations, gives entrance into the everyday world of history making in a way that no other research method can offer.

## Life Narratives

I was at a conference of anthropologists about a decade ago when I ran into a colleague who had previously done research in Panama. After a brief conversation about my work in Loma Bonita – at that time about four decades old – he asked, "Aren't you bored after so much time studying in one small place, in one small country?"

No, I wasn't at all bored. To the contrary, as I've mentioned, I was still fascinated by my ongoing academic journey in the community. But my colleague's question did unveil my unmet yearning to share Loma Bonita's historical experience with a wider audience than in the past. I had published a number of articles and a book, all written in the traditional academic style, but none had conveyed the very thing that had kept me hooked to my fieldwork all these years: the people of Loma Bonita, themselves; their stubborn will to keep struggling despite umpteen strikes against them; their joys and sorrows, humor and ire, despair and hope. I wanted to make these people come alive for readers.

I resolved to write about Loma Bonita's history in a more heartfelt way, through the life story of Esperanza Ruiz and her family, individuals whose paths I'd been following over decades. People I knew well. By presenting a close-up view of their lives, I hoped that readers would be better able to imagine "the individual in history, and history in the individual."[4] This was not a new idea. The study of individual lives as a means to understand their broader cultural or historical context has deep roots in anthropology, dating back at least a century. In the early 1900s, while many US anthropologists were studying Indigenous peoples[5] in order to classify their cultural "traits," one young anthropologist, Paul Radin, was instead spending time listening to the life stories of individuals from the Winnebago tribe.[6] His 1926 autobiography of a Winnebago man named Crashing Thunder became one of the most well-known life narratives of the period, and encouraged other anthropologists to use this life history genre.

Most of the autobiographical studies that followed Radin's lead were (like most other anthropological works) by and about men, treating Indigenous women only in passing and primarily as wives and mothers.[7] An exception came in 1961 with the publication of anthropologist Nancy Lurie's autobiography of Mountain Wolf Woman, the Winnebago sister of Crashing Thunder. For five months, Mountain Wolf Woman sat in Lurie's home in Michigan and tape-recorded an account of her 75 years of life. She emerged in the book as a self-confident, self-reliant woman; a gatherer and gardener of food; and a major economic player in control of her household income and finances.[8] As one book reviewer noted,[9] this autobiography stood almost alone at the time as a description of an Indigenous woman living a full life in her own sphere.

For about two decades after the publication of Mountain Wolf Woman, there was a lull in research using life narratives in anthropology.[10] But beginning in the 1980s, under the influence of feminist and postmodernist ideas, the study of individual lives through life histories and autobiographies came roaring back.[11]

Like Lurie before them, feminist anthropologists of a new generation were bent on addressing the discipline's past failure to document women's lives fully. Some turned to studies of individual women as one way to show the importance, diversity, and complexity of their roles and experiences. Among the spate of unforgettable Latin American women we meet in these life histories during the 1980s and 1990s are Rigoberta Menchú,[12] an Indigenous Guatemalan woman and political leader who narrated her story as a way to expose her government's atrocities against her people and who later won a Nobel Peace Prize; Esperanza Hernández,[13] a Mexican street peddler whose "fighting strength" was a major theme of her life and who later would be the subject of a theater production based on the book; and Sofía Velasquez,[14] a "plucky" Bolivian market vender, union leader, and worker of magic, who would also become the subject of a video about her life.[15]

At the same time, a new generation of anthropologists swayed by postmodernist ideas began experimenting with innovative types of life narratives that give centrality in their research and writing to the effects of the researcher's own biography (a process referred to as "self-reflexivity"). One form, referred to as "autoethnography,"[16] typically includes the personal story of the anthropologist as part of the study of others, and aims to lay bare the emotional attachments involved in the research process. Ruth Behar, for example, intertwined her own story as a Cuban American with that of the Mexican street peddler whose life she documented. In other studies in this genre, anthropologists examine their own ethnic or minority groups, including their own lives in the mix.

Another more recent experimental type of life narrative, called "intimate ethnography," has roots in ideas from feminist, postmodernist, and Marxist anthropology. In this genre, the research spotlight is not on the anthropologist but on someone with whom the anthropologist has an intimate personal relation. Alisse Waterston,[17] for instance, presents the life history of her father as a means to analyze the nature of global violence in the twentieth century and its effects on individual human lives.

I've taken inspiration for this book from all of these fresh currents of life narrative. Like many feminist life histories and intimate ethnographies, Esperanza's story examines her life as a window to understanding how specific historical changes affect the daily experiences of real people. And similar to each type of life narrative mentioned, this book attempts to honor the emotional dimension of Esperanza's relationships, and of my connection to her and her family.

But in one major way, this life story differs from them all.

## The Life Narrative of Esperanza and Her Family

Most anthropologists have learned about a person's life story by sitting with that person for one (or many) interview sessions[18] and, with recorder turned on, saying, "Tell me about your life." They may or may not pose specific questions to guide the life narrative.[19] This method asks the person being interviewed, frequently a community elder, to look as far back in time as possible. It's a research approach that elicits fascinating accounts of lives lived, narrated often with insight and zest. But relying on only a single person's account can raise questions about historical accuracy. What if that man's memory has faded or that woman has intentionally colored the past in ways that wrongly depict her or others? Or what if they each have invented experiences just to please their interviewer? Questions like these leave further corroboration of the narrative to the anthropologist who may or may not be in a position to investigate veracity.

This study of Esperanza's life takes a different methodological approach to learning about her past and present. I never did sit down with her and ask that she narrate her life story, and truthfully, I have no idea what she might have told me had I tried. Instead, I've drawn on my long-term participant observation research to reconstruct the life history of this woman and those of members of four generations of her family.

Esperanza and I have always come together as anthropologist and research subject, but from the very beginning, we've also simply been two women who love the telling and the listening that make for lively conversations, and, with time and trust, the exchange of personal tales. This happened often after breakfast, when the rest of the family had left for the day's work or school. We'd be alone, sitting on low benches, face to face and close up, swapping stories while perhaps separating beans from their pods on the wooden trays sitting in our laps. At other times, memories flowed as we climbed down to Copé to buy supplies or attend a political meeting or traveled together to visit her children in the city. We also had "real" interviews, sometimes taped or recorded digitally, when I would question her, as I would every adult in the community, about a particular topic: her work history or family genealogy, her political or religious perspectives.

My developing bond with Esperanza nourished my relationships with her immediate family. Easily so. That we all saw one another twice a day for a sit-down meal requiring conversation and humor gave us a greater level of comfort than I had with any other family. Esperanza's husband soon became my ally, and their five children took cues from their parents, quickly engaging with me as someone to talk and laugh with as well as to help out with her work.

All the stories they've told me and the experiences we've shared in the course of my 50 years of fieldwork and 20 research visits have made their way into my fieldnotes, interviews, recordings, computer files, and photos. Out of this mountain of documents and memories comes this life narrative.

Basing Esperanza's life story on my half-century of field research, rather than on her retrospective account of her life, brings losses and gains. Lost is access to her own memory of her past, to what she would have remembered (or not) about her life at the time of the interview(s). Gained, besides a high degree of immediacy, are three main advantages that come from my having been present in the community, either as eyewitness to events in Esperanza's life or with access to others who were there. Either way, I'd be scrupulously recording what she and others said, did, and told me they thought.

The first of these three advantages is an improved chance at understanding how Esperanza experienced events back when they were happening. The second is my ability to view her not only as an individual but as a member of a community and family, with many of the complex interactions and emotions such neighbor and kin relationships entail. The third advantage to basing Esperanza's life narrative on my 50 years of participant observation rather than on retrospective interviews alone is that I could record the smallest details of a story through time, which might reveal patterns and connections not otherwise apparent. Keep these three advantages in mind as you read this story about Esperanza and four generations of her family.

Of course, long-term participant observation, like any social research method, has many limitations. What I've learned from Esperanza and her family, and inscribed in this book, represents only a partial reality – the part I chose to pursue while doing fieldwork and writing about it, and the part that she and her family chose to reveal to me. Moreover, some stories that I originally included had to be revised or eliminated at their request: in 2019, with a first draft of this book in hand, I sat down with Esperanza and each of her five children, in turn, to translate what I'd written about them and ask their permission for its inclusion. What I offer, therefore, is an imperfect moving picture of their family life but one, I hope, that is enlightening and memorable.

## Writing

Out of bits and pieces of my half-century of collected interviews and fieldnotes documenting my experiences of and conversations about and with Esperanza and her family, I've woven a full cloth for this book. As I worked on the writing, I kept my purposes steadfastly before me. Aside from telling the story of Esperanza and her family in a way that would shed light on a century of change in their community and wider world, I wanted to try to capture and hold my readers' attention. This meant writing a relatively short book that, as much as possible, "showed" history through stories rather than "told" it through lectures.

And me? I'm shamelessly very present in this book, as chief narrator and explainer, the person who gives facts and figures to provide some local-to-global context. And, after 1972, I appear as a character in some of the scenes. I'm also present behind the curtain, the person who decided which stories to include in the book, how to present them, and in what order. But despite my presence in these obvious and subtler ways, this book is about them, not me. I've intentionally limited anything relevant about my own story to the introduction and conclusion in order to privilege what I think matters most: this woman and her family, the people of Loma Bonita, and the history of them all.

To frame this history, here's a glance at the wider Panamanian world into which Esperanza would be born.

# 1

# The Isthmus of Panama: Two Different Worlds (pre-1920s)

*More than five centuries ago, Spaniards invaded the Isthmus of Panama. They built a road across a narrow stretch of land in the middle of the isthmus that connected the Atlantic and Pacific Oceans, and this road – this "transit zone" – became a seat of wealth and power linked closely to the globalizing capitalist world economy. In control of Panama's transit zone and its riches were Panama's commercial classes, and, through time, a series of foreign powers: Spain, Colombia, and finally the United States after 1903 when it built the Panama Canal and created its own center of might, the "Canal Zone."*

*The rest of the isthmus, the "interior," is where most Panamanians, including the people of Loma Bonita, have lived as poor subsistence farmers during these centuries. Their separate world would not even be linked to the transit zone by a paved highway until the 1940s.*

## IN THE BEGINNING

It might have been as long ago as 15 million years when a narrow strip of dry land emerged from below the ocean waters, creating a land bridge for the very first time between what had been two separate continents – North and South America.[1] This was the Isthmus of Panama, a ribbon of beautiful, mountainous land that formed a link between two continents and separated two oceans – the Atlantic and Pacific (see Map 1).

If you had made your way to this isthmus about 13,500 years ago, you could have found people moving from place to place who subsisted by hunting animals and gathering plants.[2] They were the first humans that archaeologists have documented to have been living on the isthmus. The archaeological record shows that about 9,500 years ago some of these Indigenous peoples had added cultivated crops, like **arrowroot** and later squash, to their diet, but it wasn't until 7,000 years later – about 2,200 years ago – that some had settled down in large permanent farming villages. There they planted crops like corn, **yuca**, squash, and yams and traded their goods with different communities and regions. Through time, their settlements increased and populations grew. By 500 years ago, the isthmus was home to a rich diversity of cultures, and as many as a million people.[3] Legend has it that the name Panama meant "land of abundant fish" in the language of one of these Indigenous peoples.

## A SHATTERED WORLD

Then suddenly their world was shattered. Spaniards landed on the Atlantic coast of the isthmus beginning in 1501 and began their assault on the Indigenous population. The first Spanish governor, nicknamed "Pedrarias the Cruel" for his atrocities, promoted their massacre, rape, robbery, and enslavement.[4] Many Indigenous groups organized, fought back fiercely, and won battles. One legendary leader of this resistance, Urracá, was from the mountains of central Panama, not far from Loma Bonita's region today. He organized leaders of the area to fight against the Spaniards in Coclé's lowland town of Natá, which he and his fighters successfully attacked several times, burning it to the ground in 1529. Urracá's ending is also legendary; although the Spanish did manage to trap and capture him, he escaped their clutches and got back to his home village in the mountains where he continued the rebellion until he died free from Spanish captivity in 1531.[5] Unfortunately, Urracá's fate was not shared by most of the Indigenous peoples in that western, most populated area of the isthmus. By 1522, as much as 93 percent of the population there had perished in what Panamanian historian Castillero Calvo refers to as a "holocaust."[6] They were overrun by Spanish brutality and more advanced military technology, and by European diseases against which they had no immunities.[7]

Many of those who did manage to survive the conquest and its aftermath escaped from Spanish control in the Pacific lowlands by fleeing into the nearby mountains. There they joined or formed small communities of kin who worked the land as subsistence farmers, providing their own food and basic needs. Meanwhile, back down in the lowlands, Spaniards who were now short of exploitable workers turned to importing enslaved Africans and forced laborers from elsewhere to build their towns and work their mines, cattle ranches, and agricultural plantations.

One day in September of 1513, a Spanish governor named Vasco Núñez de Balboa climbed onto a mountaintop in Panama and saw something amazing. Balboa had been leading an expedition of several hundred men trekking south from the Atlantic side of the isthmus through dense jungles, rivers, and swamps. Their mission was to find gold and also a "new sea" that Indigenous people had told them existed to the south. From high up on his perch on that day, Balboa sighted that "South Sea" – the Pacific Ocean – and soon claimed it in the name of the Spanish Crown.[8] This discovery would shape a unique history for the Isthmus of Panama.

## TRANSIT ZONE VERSUS INTERIOR

The knowledge that Panama provided a short "bridge" between the two oceans led the Spanish Crown during the 1520s to build a narrow stone "Royal Road" (Camino Real) across the isthmus, connecting the Atlantic and Pacific oceans. At the Pacific end they established Panama City. On the Atlantic coast they founded other ports that enabled them to ship the silver they had mined in South America (Peru and Bolivia) up the Pacific coast to Panama City to be carried by slaves and mules across the isthmus along the "Royal Road" and then loaded on ships to Spain. Once there, goods went to other European countries, and ultimately China. From then on, Panama's "**transit zone**" between its Pacific and Atlantic coasts became a center of vast wealth, tied tightly to the nascent global capitalist economy. A small, enormously wealthy class of white Spaniards in Panama City controlled this highly profitable commerce and held great power on the isthmus. Their riches came from ownership of multiple business enterprises, especially transportation and real estate services connected to the transit zone. Some also owned cattle ranches and/or ships with slaves aboard to fish for valuable pearls in the Gulf of Panama.[9]

Outside of this busy transit zone lay the rest of Panama, referred to as the "**interior**," an entirely different world.[10] Most of the isthmian population lived in this predominantly rural region, some under the authority of Spaniards in small lowland towns, cattle ranches, and plantations, or as laborers in their mines. Others were descendants of those Indigenous people or slaves who had escaped Spanish domination to live as independent subsistence farmers whose lives were unrelated to the ups and downs of Panama's globalizing economy in the transit zone. They were able to maintain this agricultural way of life because rural Panama offered them an abundance of available land. Unlike in other Central American countries where Spanish **oligarchs** held power by controlling the land, in Panama, the wealth of most oligarchs was linked to the urban transit zone. Most land in Panama's interior, therefore, continued to be owned by the faraway Spanish Crown, which freely granted poor farmers "use rights," though not legal ownership, to land in which Spain had no interest.[11]

The year 1739 marks the opening saga in a long-term period of change in Coclé Province. That year, the British attacked and destroyed Panama's Atlantic port of Portobelo, triggering the decline of the isthmus as an international trading route and a century-long economic depression.[12] This severe economic downturn in the transit zone led some of Panama City's prosperous merchant families to leave the capital[13] and move into nearby Coclé Province (see Map 2) where they divided up the Pacific lowlands into large cattle farms.[14] Although this left many poorer lowland farmers without enough land for their livelihood, they were able to continue farming by moving up to more remote parts of the nearby mountains where public (Crown) lands were available for their use. One such farmer was a young woman named Reina Ruiz who, according to genealogies I collected, made this move up to an almost unpopulated area of Coclé's Pacific mountains and settled in a place (today) called Loma Bonita. Reina was the great-great-grandmother of Esperanza Ruiz, whom I would meet many years later.[15]

## FOREIGN IMPERIALISM: SPAIN, COLOMBIA, AND THE UNITED STATES OF AMERICA

The separate and differing worlds of poor interior farmers and transit zone urbanites continued to characterize Panama's story during three centuries of Spanish colonial rule. Nor did this change after 1821 when Panama declared its independence from Spain and joined a political federation with Colombia.[16] As one of Colombia's "departments" under this alliance, Panama was officially governed by those in power in distant Bogotá. In reality, however, the autonomy of the isthmus's elite merchant class in Panama City ebbed and flowed as power shifted between Colombia's Liberal and Conservative parties.[17] Back and forth swung the political pendulum throughout the nineteenth century as these parties battled for control, bringing times of democratic or authoritarian rule, of peace or violent conflicts, of foreign interventions or domestic control. Particularly important for Panama were economic booms in the transit zone in both the 1850s, when New York City capitalists funded a railroad across the Isthmus of Panama, and the 1880s, when the French tried (but failed) to build a canal.[18]

Despite these swings of the pendulum through time, one thing never changed: the attention and resources of those in power – either in Bogotá or in Panama – and among interested foreigners remained focused on Panama's transit zone, not its interior. There was still not even a good road linking these two parts of the isthmus at the beginning of the twentieth century when Panama's fate was once again about to be transformed.[19]

In 1903, the United States sent warships to Panama to help a group of Panamanian elites win isthmian independence from Colombia in exchange for the right to build and control a canal.[20] The United States did build its Panama Canal between 1907 and 1914, a waterway that zigzagged across the isthmus for about 80 kilometers (50 miles), linking the Atlantic and Pacific Oceans. But the new Panamanian Republic did not gain real independence. The Panama Canal Treaty of 1903 (that no

Panamanian ever saw or signed)[21] and the new Panama constitution of 1904 turned the isthmus into a virtual colony of the United States, dominated to an extent unrivaled in the hemisphere. The United States got authority over the Panama Canal "in perpetuity," as well as a "Canal Zone" that was about 8 kilometers (5 miles) wide on each side of the canal. Included within this "Zone" was the old Spanish "Royal Road" and transit zone. Only the two cities at each end of the Canal Zone (Colón on the Atlantic side and Panama City on the Pacific) remained in Panama's jurisdiction.

Adding insult to injury for Panamanians, the Canal Zone was organized as an apartheid-like colonial enclave. To maintain control of this area and assure that it served US interests, the US government depopulated and dismantled the places where Panamanians had previously lived and worked,[22] replacing them with new military bases, towns, and communities for US personnel and canal workers. The Zone had its own US-controlled schools, post offices, stores, ports, police force, and government. In this official US territory, white workers from the United States earned much more than Panamanians and other non-US laborers,[23] and they alone got to live in lovely, well-maintained houses with manicured lawns.

Nor was domination confined to the Canal Zone; the United States gained implicit veto power over Panamanian actions it considered contrary to its interests.[24] US banks, corporations, and the US government held sway over the economy, even adopting the US dollar as Panama's currency.[25] So tight was US economic control that Panamanians were not permitted to construct railroads, highways, or means of communication without US approval. And the US military gained a tight grasp on the new country; by one estimate,[26] the United States invaded or intervened in Panamanian affairs at least 16 times between 1856 and 1925, often to put down social unrest and rebellion among the popular classes.

Far from the hustle and bustle of this transit zone in the early 1920s was Panama's rural interior, still a different world with no decent road connecting the two regions. Overland trails in the interior disappeared in rain and mud during a good part of the year, while travel by small steamboat or sailboat to the transit zone was expensive and time consuming, dependent on prevailing winds and weather. But a possible change was on the horizon. By the 1920s, some members of Panama's commercial classes sought to overcome US control of transportation and communications by building a road that would link the transit zone with the interior, and stimulate business for their own benefit. Construction began in 1922 along the Pacific coast in Coclé Province and reached Panama City in 1926.[27] But it was still a rough, unfinished gravel road that was impassible during parts of the eight-month rainy season; I've been told that the 193-kilometer (120-mile) car ride from Coclé's lowland town of **Penonomé** to the capital took 12 hours in the 1920s.

It was on a rainy Thursday in November of 1922, while this road was under construction in Coclé's Pacific lowlands, that high up in the nearby mountains baby Esperanza Ruiz first opened her eyes.

It's time to let Esperanza speak.

# 2

# Childhood: As Soon As I Opened My Eyes (1920s–1930s)

*When Esperanza Ruiz was a child, the United States had completed the Panama Canal and solidified its power over the isthmus. But Esperanza never laid eyes on the canal or Panama City, never knew anything about the globalized world of the transit zone. Her happiness and sadness, fears and hopes were pinned to the world of Loma Bonita and the nearby mountains.*

*This was life in a rural subsistence economy, during a time when land was abundant and provided families with most of what they needed for their livelihoods. It was a time when people had few material possessions but an abundance of kin and neighbors all around to share burdens and joys, and to provide a measure of economic security and control over the rhythm of life.*

## 1922 – WELCOME ESPERANZA

On her knees, holding tightly onto the rope hanging from the rafters, Natalia Ruiz makes a final push and gives birth to a baby girl, her first child. Natalia's aunt is right there to cut the cord and clean and swaddle baby Esperanza. It's late November 1922 during the height of the rainy season. Sheets of water pound the red tile roof of this one-room adobe home belonging to Natalia's parents, Natividad Ruiz and Benita Herrera. Outside in the nearby kitchen, with its thatch roof and cane walls, Natalia's mother and two sisters are discussing every detail of the successful birth as they boil water on the woodstove. They're preparing the cornbread and chicken that will be the mainstay of Natalia's diet for the next 40 days. Yuca, their usual staple, is mostly out during this delicate time. Natalia and baby Esperanza will stay inside the house for 7 days, and then very nearby for the next 33.

There are evil forces that threaten the lives of new mothers and babies in Loma Bonita. So Natalia's older sister wraps a piece of red string around baby Esperanza's left wrist and right ankle to keep her shielded from witches and the evil eye (people who could cause her harm by simply looking or laughing at her). Natalia also will protect herself during the next 40 days by placing cotton in her ears, a cloth around her forehead, and a hat on her head. Her mother will help her heal from childbirth with a daily sponge bath from the leaves of several local plants.[1]

Baby Esperanza joins a large household of 10 members, including her 21-year-old mother Natalia and her mother's parents, brother, and three unmarried sisters, one with three young children living in the house. Esperanza's father, Manuel Blanco, is not part of this birth scene, although he lives on a nearby slope in Loma Bonita. He's married to her mother's older sister, Marta, and, although he doesn't deny paternity, he refuses to recognize Esperanza formally and take on responsibilities. Natalia's mother (and Esperanza's grandmother), Benita, says she's sorry that Manuel "took advantage of young Natalia, but that's all done now, and baby Esperanza seems healthy." Natalia and her baby will stay here in her parents' home for as long as she wants, just like her sister is doing with her three children. This is a commonplace arrangement in Loma Bonita when one parent, either the young mother or father, does not want to live with the other. No agreement, no public union.[2] There are no legal or economic stumbling blocks to a girl's staying with her parents, and no social shame. Esperanza will use her mother's surname, "Ruiz," as is customary.

Natalia spends the baby's first few months in her parents' home, but it turns out that their stay isn't long. A suitor in whom Natalia is interested starts showing up at the house. Teodoro Ruiz, a distant cousin, lets Natalia and her parents know that he wants to live together and recognize Esperanza as his daughter. Natalia likes his light skin and blue eyes, a characteristic of some people in his family, but Teodoro has no land of his own; in an unusual move, his father had sold all his land to an uncle years ago and then left Loma Bonita to live elsewhere. Manuel Blanco, Esperanza's biological father, provides a solution by offering

Natalia and Teodoro a plot of his land on which to build a house "so that the baby girl can have a place to live." And, Esperanza's grandfather, Natividad, helps by promising to lend them enough land to plant the food crops they'll need to feed their family. Natalia decides to accept this union, and she and Teodoro build a one-room adobe house up the slope from where Manuel and Marta live. Esperanza is six months old when they move into their new house.

**BOX 2.1 A WIDER LENS: DIVERSE ANCESTRIES IN THE PANAMANIAN POPULATION**

Teodoro's light skin and blue eyes were rare but not unique in this rural region. The descendants of Reina Ruiz, like other Panamanians, were *mestizas/os*, combining Indigenous, African, and European ancestries. Panama's history had forged this distinct mix beginning in the sixteenth century with "encounters" between Indigenous peoples, the Spanish invaders, and the large numbers of slaves and forced laborers the Spaniards imported from Africa and other Latin American countries. Then during the nineteenth and early twentieth century, the French and US foreigners who financed the railroad and two canals imported almost all workers from the Caribbean islands and China, with some also from Colombia and Europe.[3]

This history produced a diverse, predominantly black populace in Panama. Interestingly, recent linguistic and genetic studies of the country's entire population have revealed that below the surface of this diversity lies a persistent influence of Indigenous peoples on Panama's genetic pool. This research indicates that over 80 percent of contemporary Panamanians carry a maternal heritage that is exclusively Indigenous; in contrast, their male genetic heritage is more European and African.[4] These patterns fit what we know about the early decades of the Spanish conquest in Panama. The current preponderance of female Indigenous genes could be linked to the fact that the Spanish invaders, almost entirely men, frequently raped Indigenous women or cohabited with them – be the women willing or not. The less prominent contribution of Indigenous male genes to Panama's population today is likely related to the very high death rate of Indigenous men, compared to women, during the devastating wars with Spaniards.

## A LIFE SURROUNDED BY KIN

"What's the first thing you remember as a little girl," I once asked Esperanza.

> As soon as I opened my eyes, I saw these mountains and all of my relatives. They were always there, like that huge rock near the stream.

Everyone Esperanza talked to or played or worked with when she was a child was a relative. In her own home, she had three sisters and four brothers by her late teens. Not far down the slopes lived Aunt Marta with Papa Manuel, a house that eventually included 10 first cousins. Another two of her mother's siblings lived not far away, adding 20 more first cousins to her everyday life. And, a walk down the slopes got Esperanza to her grandparents' house where she was born and where other aunts, uncles, and cousins lived.

These closest relatives formed the core of Esperanza's world, but she also shared kinship with someone in every one of the other 11 or 12 households in Loma Bonita. This tight kinship web traced back to one woman, Reina Ruiz, who, as I've mentioned (Chapter 1), was among the first permanent settlers in Loma Bonita in the 1830s or 40s. Back when Reina and some family members first arrived in this sparsely populated region, the land was still public, owned by the government; Reina's family could claim "use rights" to as much as was needed. Genealogies show that, over time, Reina had ten children (with two men), eight of whom (five daughters and three sons) later married someone from a nearby community and brought them to live in Loma Bonita. In this way, the community grew, with ample land for crops and cattle available for all. When Reina died in the early twentieth century, every household in Loma Bonita included at least one of her descendants. Esperanza's grandfather, Natividad, was her grandson, making Esperanza, as I've noted, her great-great-granddaughter. According to Esperanza's mother, Natalia, the house where Esperanza was born was very close to where Reina had raised her family.

## SUBSISTENCE FARMING WHEN LAND WAS ABUNDANT

Like her great-great-grandmother, and later her mother, Esperanza grew up in a family of subsistence farmers who got most of what they needed to eat and live from the land they farmed and the animals they raised. They practiced swidden agriculture, a type of farming adapted to the tropical weather pattern that shaped their lives. When the rains stopped in January, Esperanza's grandfather, Natividad, would offer her parents a plot of ***monte*** (forest land used to plant food crops). With his machete, her stepfather Teodoro would cut down the trees and brush on this plot, and leave it all on the ground to dry thoroughly during the upcoming three-month dry, hot summer. Then, right before the rains began again in April or May, he and Natalia would burn the now-dried, crisp brush so they could plant right in the ashes using a digging stick, a long wood pole with a pointed end. Once or twice before the harvest, they'd return to weed these fields. For two years in a row, they'd farm this same plot but then leave it to rest and regenerate for as long as 15 or 20 years. After each two-year cycle, therefore, Esperanza's grandfather had to provide her parents with a new piece of land to work.

Natalia and Teodoro were partners in this agricultural life. In those days, men were primarily responsible for the work of cutting down the trees and brush, while men and women both had a hand in burning, planting, weeding, and harvesting their crops (see Figure 2.1). Once food was harvested, women did much of the processing and cooking. The reality, though, was that family circumstances often influenced who did each job. Natalia, for example, had six sisters but only one brother, so in her family, girls helped with most work in their *monte*. Even for jobs usually assigned to one gender, there was plenty of flexibility; young women sometimes did cut down the trees and brush, and men helped often with household tasks like husking rice.

Pointing to her *monte* one day, Natalia told me, "This land gives us life; it's like our mother." Land was the source of everyone's livelihood as well as their home when Esperanza was a child, and women and men had equal rights by law to use it and then pass it on for others to use. It also was abundant, so all families had at least enough access to land to meet most of their basic subsistence needs. Although the Panamanian government was still the legal owner of almost all land in that highland region in the 1920s, community members – like Reina Ruiz a century before – could assert their "use rights" by clearing an unclaimed forest plot, reporting it to the local government official (*regidor*), and cultivating it for as long as needed.[5]

**Figure 2.1. Harvesting corn in *monte*, 1993. Photo by Reid R. Frazier.**

In 1972, Esperanza's biological father, Manuel Blanco, described that land situation this way:

> At that time, we were poor, without money. We didn't wear shoes or have decent clothing or elegant houses or hospitals and schools, or even a church. But we all had enough land to grow most of our food, and there was wood, good wood, nearby. Everywhere you looked there was forest, pure forest, and the rivers and streams in these parts were rich with fish, and wild pigs and iguanas roamed these hills.

The most important food crops were corn, beans, yuca, and rice, but families planted smaller amounts of many things, like yams, *guandú*

**Figure 2.2. Chopping wood for stove, 1979.**

(pigeon peas), *otoe* (taro), sugarcane, bananas, plantains, cocoa, coconuts, coffee, gourds, and fruits such as oranges, mangos, and guava. For protein, everyone raised chickens, and some, like Esperanza's grandparents, had cows, horses, and pigs. "Nothing went to waste," Natalia explained:

> We cut wood from the forest nearby to build our houses and furniture and to cook food [Figure 2.2], and we used the clays all around here for our houses and cooking utensils. We grew trees for gourds to carve containers for water and for cups and spoons. With grasses from close by, we made baskets and ropes, thatching for our houses, and woven hats to wear and sell. We grew lots of sugarcane to use as food for our animals and also to sweeten coffee or make candy, corn beer, and other liquors. And our animals gave us fats for cooking and for medicines and soap. Everywhere there were plants we could use for medicines.

There were "lean times" in Loma Bonita, especially in June and July before the harvest, but, as Esperanza recalled, "Although in those months we sometimes had nights when we went to bed without enough food – just a little, old, stringy yuca – I can't remember any time when we had nothing at all to eat."

In those lean months of June and July, men would also go hunting to supplement the food supply. Manuel Blanco reminisced enthusiastically about long-distance hunting forays when he'd cross the Continental Divide from the Pacific side to get to "the other [Atlantic] side."

> When there wasn't much work to do in our fields, my brother and I would travel for days [by foot] to "the other side" to hunt wild pigs and deer and bring meat back home. Sometimes we'd bring rubber that we got from the trees there, or turtle oil to sell or use as medicine. We loved being there.

## COOPERATION WHEN YOU CAN'T DO IT ALONE

But having access to enough land didn't guarantee enough food. "No one could do it alone," Esperanza explained. "You needed help from your relatives and neighbors":

> My house was like one big family with my grandparents and with the families of Mama's two sisters who lived near us. We children were always running back and forth between our aunts' houses to deliver or borrow things like yuca or salt. Sometimes in the morning our woodstove would be cold because the log Mama had left lit for the night had stopped burning. Mama would send me running to Aunt Marta's to get a match. My grandparents had cows, and we didn't, so we'd get some milk or cheese or meat from them, and they came to us for molasses or for us to work for a day in their fields.

Members of these four households shared labor regularly as well as food. When one family needed help, someone from another would come work for a day. They could earn a day's labor, to be reciprocated in the future, or, instead, take home part of what they harvested. Esperanza remembered that people could also work for things other than labor and food.

> Once I worked for my grandmother harvesting yuca for the afternoon in exchange for a beautiful piece of cloth. I also remember

> helping my grandfather plant rice for *un real* [5¢] a day, plus I got fed two great meals with meat, and they gave me corn to take home to make ***bollos*** [corn buns].

These various ways of exchanging labor between close kin and neighbors were key to survival for Loma Bonita families. But this still didn't solve their need for an even larger labor force to do certain heavy jobs, like cutting down the bush or building a house, or for work that had to be done quickly, such as burning, planting, and harvesting. That's when a family would organize a *junta*.

Family members would invite people from one house or five or six houses to come work for a day. In exchange, workers got one or two meals and homemade corn beer at the end of that day. Then, the "owners" of the *junta* owed all those people a future day of labor.

As a child, Esperanza loved going to *juntas*. She told me,

> Everyone would be there: my grandparents, uncles, aunts, and a ton of cousins. Some, but not all, of the women would stay at the house to cook big delicious meals, chicken or beef with rice usually, and to weave hats, while the other women and the men would go to plant the rice or whatever. While they worked, you could hear those people contentedly shouting their "calls" [*gritos*] from far away. Children usually stayed back at the house. Unless we were fighting or got hurt, no one paid us much attention, and we'd climb trees and play games like hide-and-seek and hopscotch.
>
> Afterwards, the adults would come back to the house for lots of food and corn beer. Those men could drink a gallon each. It was very festive; they would dance ***tamborito*** all night long while women sang and clapped and several men played the drums.

*Juntas* were not just a time to get agricultural work done. They were one of the main ways for people to socialize, have fun, or quarrel. Often, there was lots of drama. Men and women had flings together, and boys and girls flirted. Esperanza reminisced,

> As a young teenager, I was short and the only girl who was fat. And I had bad hair that grew only to my chest. But I had a pretty face because I was young, and at *juntas* I flirted with the boys as much as any girl.

*Juntas* were also a time when adults, more often men than women, became emboldened or enfeebled by corn beer and fought – with words or machetes. I've heard of cases when a man lost an eye or part of a leg or his life during a *junta*. Esperanza recalled,

> Once when I was a small girl, my two uncles got into a fight about land at a *junta* at our house. They were very, very drunk and could hardly stand. Uncle Leonel cut Uncle Simon's ear with his machete, and then Simon got Leonel's hand. There was so much blood that Uncle Leonel had to be carried in a hammock to a healer a half-hour climb away. I was terrified to watch this. Uncle Leonel never could use his hand well after that, and they both went to jail for a while.

## SCHOOL AT LAST, WITH SOME DOWNSIDES

In one key way Esperanza's life differed from her mother's. In 1921, the Panamanian government responded to local petitions and established the first primary school in Loma Bonita; children from four contiguous communities would eventually attend three grades.

Before then, most people in this community and the region did not know how to read or write. Manuel Blanco, born in 1885, described himself in 1972 this way:

> I'm ignorant. I don't know how to read or write or anything. I only know how to converse. Because at that time there was no school around here. Now there are schools everywhere. Everyone is opening their eyes.

For people in and near Loma Bonita, the presence of a school was momentous. Community members organized to build a small schoolhouse with a place for a teacher to sleep during the school week. Esperanza's mother, Natalia, told me about "those exciting days."

> We all helped. The community's *regidor* organized our work. The men here already had their *faena* [a work group of men over 18 years old who were required by the government to provide three days labor a year to clear community paths and the cemetery]. So now these men

> also had to build the school. We women came to help thatch the roof and walls. And we brought water and food for the men and the teacher. Each month a different family provided the food for the workers, and we started having meetings for parents with children in the school.

By the time Esperanza started school in 1930, Loma Bonita had its own one-room school building with adobe walls, a cement floor, and a metal roof. I asked her what she remembered about her school days.

> Well, I remember that I was often late because I had morning chores. I'd climb down to fetch water from the stream and then feed the chickens. Oh, how those chickens would come running when I tossed out the corn and imitated Mama's call, *whoopie, pollito, pollito.* Then Mama would braid my hair and fetch my dress from above the woodstove.

The trip to school, said Esperanza, wasn't easy:

> I had to cross five streams, and it could be dangerous, especially when it rained. At the first stream I'd usually meet up with my cousins Felipa and Bianca, and not be alone.
>
> What I remember about school was that the teacher made us repeat the same thing over and over and over; it could be very boring. Truthfully, I liked recess the best; Felipa, Bianca, and I would find a corner to play jacks.

Mostly, what Esperanza remembered was the walk home after school. "We were all so happy. We'd walk slowly and look for fruits to eat and crabs to catch in the stream for dinner. Those crabs really loved the rain."

The walk home could also get dramatic. Esperanza described numerous fights between kids, especially between her cousins Felipa and Monica.

> Those two girls were always fighting. Right there on the road, they'd take off their dresses and yell and push each other until someone older pulled them apart or the rain started. Then they'd throw those dresses back on, and we'd all run home. Keeping those dresses clean was important. The clothing we girls wore back then was whatever cloth was lying around. So you usually had only one decent dress for school.

> Sometimes after those fights, I'd get home late, and Mama would be mad. The first thing she'd say was, "Esperanza, get that dress off you right now," and she'd hang it over the woodstove to dry. Then she'd scold me, and sometimes hit me here on my leg.

"Did your mother often hit you?" I asked. "No, not often," she responded, "but sometimes hard, with the strap. Back then, Gloria, it was customary to teach children this way, to help them learn respect for elders and hard work." I continued, "Did anyone else hit you when you were young?"

> My [step]father. Papa Teodoro sometimes even slapped my face hard. And my grandfather Natividad, too. He was a tall, thin man who was quick to get angry and scold people. He would yell at us kids and hit us. I was afraid of him. Once I went to his house to help grind their sugarcane and take some home to Mama. By mistake I dropped the big gourd that had the juice in it. It was an accident, but he hit me anyway.
>
> Grandmother Benita wasn't like him. She'd scold me sometimes, and say, "Esperanza, don't hold the machete like that," but she never hit me. She had a different way to teach us. She was wonderful with us grandchildren, and we all loved her. Although quite bent over, she was pretty, with very wavy hair, light brown eyes, and white skin; they say her family had some Spanish blood.

## CATHOLICISM WITHOUT CHURCH OR PRIEST

Like everyone else in Loma Bonita in the 1920s and 30s, Esperanza's family members considered themselves to be Catholic. Since there were no priests, churches, or chapels nearby, they practiced their faith in community-led prayer meetings in people's homes.

One of Esperanza's earliest memories was when her baby sister died. "It was parasites that took her," Esperanza told me, "although Mama thought she was killed by evil eye."

> I was only four or five years old, but I remember the walk down the slopes with Mama to my grandparents' house. Mama was

> carrying my little sister's body. They put candles all around her, and all afternoon and night everyone from Loma Bonita came to pray. That night the men built a little wooden box for my sister. At first light the next morning, some grownups went down to our cemetery to dig the grave hole, and about noon others carried the box down to the cemetery and buried her.

People climbed down to lowland centers of church control only a few times a year. They'd go to towns in Coclé Province, like Penonomé, Natá, or Antón, to visit particular saints and ask for favors or to attend baptisms, occasional weddings, and major religious and saints' day celebrations.

Easter week was among the most important of these lowland treks. Every year, one of Esperanza's aunts and her family would leave for Penonomé at 5 a.m. on Wednesday carrying large baskets on their backs full of clothing and food. At night, they'd sleep by the roadside or with a relative or ***comadre*** who lived along the way. In Penonomé, they stayed in the home of a relative but cooked their own food separately. On Saturday, they'd start the two-day walk back to Loma Bonita.

To have a family host you for a night or two made this journey easier. But, said Esperanza, this tradition of hosting highlanders on their Easter trek to the lowlands was beginning to die out:

> Although people in the towns were hospitable to us for a while, when the older generation died, some younger ones didn't want us *cholos* [a derogatory term used by lowlanders to refer to Indigenous people and poor highlanders] in their homes. This happened to my family when the younger people in town rented their house to strangers for the week, just so they didn't have to take us in.

Other families didn't leave Loma Bonita during Easter. This was often the case for Esperanza's family:

> On Tuesday, we'd go out to gather enough wood to cook all week long. We'd stay in our house every day. We'd be sad, in mourning for the persecution of Christ. We didn't do anything because, if you used a machete, you'd be killing Christ; if you ate meat, it would be eating Christ; and people didn't have sex either. Then came Saturday, and it was joyful. If it didn't rain, it would be a day to burn our *monte* for that year.

## MONEY IN A SUBSISTENCE ECONOMY

Most things that families needed when Esperanza was young came from their *monte* and household production, their land and labor. But a few necessary or desired items had to be bought with cash. Cloth and clothing were among these expenses, although, as Esperanza's story makes clear, most people had only the barest of wardrobes and no store-bought shoes. Men typically wore tan or blue denim pants, with long-sleeved shirts of the same materials. Women's everyday outfit, called *refajo*, used similar materials. Esperanza described her mother's clothing in this way:

> Mama wrapped a large piece of heavy blue denim material around her waist (which she used as a blanket at night) and then she tied a square piece of any old cloth around her neck – front to back – and tucked it in at the waist, leaving her shoulders bare to the sun. Some women avoided this problem by wearing a blouse made of a thick white cotton material [*dril*].

For celebrations and dances, most women put on a more festive outfit, called a ***pollera***, a large, gathered skirt and blouse made from white or colorful cotton materials, often with embroidered trimming. A woman's *pollera* was important to her; Esperanza's grandmother, Benita, wore hers for her wedding and then again for her burial.

In addition to cloth and clothing, a household's short list of basic goods that had to be bought with cash in the 1920s included salt, tobacco, matches, kerosene, and machetes. I've calculated that the amount a family would have needed to pay for a year's worth of these purchases was about $20 US.[6] Although this seems like a very small sum, cash was so scarce in the highlands at that time that it took a great deal of work to earn it.

The most dependable source of money came from woven hats made primarily by the women of every household (see Figure 2.3). When Esperanza was a child, a small hat that took her mother two to three days to weave and sew sold for 10¢ in Copé. If she could have produced two hats a week on top of her other responsibilities – admittedly a difficult feat – she could have brought in about $10 a year, half of what was needed.

Where might the other half come from?

**Figure 2.3. Tina weaving hat, 2015.**

## ACCESSING MONEY: DIFFERENT FAMILIES, DIFFERENT PATHS

A few better-off families could earn needed cash through small-scale cattle trading. Esperanza's grandparents were one of only three households in Loma Bonita that owned more than 10 head of cattle in the 1920s. She remembered,

> When grandfather Natividad was young, he worked with his stepfather who would buy hats and coffee around here and take them on horseback down to a trading partner in the lowlands. This trading partner would then sell him a few head of cattle that he'd drive to Penonomé to sell to another family he knew. Later, my grandfather had his own cattle.

Natividad's only son, Dionisio (Natalia's brother), told me about the importance of cattle in the family when he was growing up:

> From the time I was a little boy, I found myself milking cows and caring for them. When I was young, about 1913 or 1910, my grandmother had 12 and her husband had 8. Papa [Natividad] had 8, and Mama [Benita], 4. You could buy a cow then for 20 or 30 pesos [$10 to $15]. Every year my parents would each kill two cows; some meat was for us to eat, and the rest they sold around Loma Bonita and in Copé. We had to kill them to buy things like clothes and matches. With that money, my father also put a metal roof on our house and bought that *trapiche* [horse-powered sugar-cane press] over there.

Most families in Loma Bonita during the 1920s didn't have enough cattle to be involved in the cattle trade, but a few tried to earn needed cash through small-scale itinerant trading. Octavio Ortiz was one of the biggest of these traders in Loma Bonita at the time. He'd sell highland-made hats, ropes, molasses, and coffee to a lowland trading partner, using the proceeds to buy a few head of cattle. Then he'd bring the animals back to Loma Bonita to slaughter and sell the meat all over the highlands.

Other families got the $10–20 they needed each year through occasional salaried work rather than trade. It had always been possible to earn small sums of cash by working for a relative or neighbor in the highlands. But no household had enough extra cash to pay adults a 10¢ to 20¢ daily wage for a sustained period of time, and there were no nearby employers. Until "Potroso."

At the end of the nineteenth century, a merchant family from Penonomé established a large coffee and cacao plantation, called Potroso, in the mountains about an hour's foot journey from Loma Bonita. Men, women, and children from the community and the region took advantage of the chance to earn cash nearby during harvest time. Neither the Ruiz's nor the Ortiz's had to do this difficult kind of work, but members of Loma Bonita's Blanco family did.

Manuel Blanco, Esperanza's biological father, started harvesting coffee and carrying wood at Potroso for 7¢ a day when he was 10 years old. His father and his mother (whom he liked to remind me had "Indian blood") also worked there at harvest time, as did his brother, Ernesto, and, years later, Ernesto's wife. In 1972, Ernesto's daughter gave me a glimpse into what Potroso meant to a poor highlander back then.

> My mother always said that this was her first real chance to improve herself. Mama would say, "Imagine that! I could make 25¢ a day. That's a *peso* [50¢] for two days work, so much more than the two *reales* [10¢] I get from selling my hat." My father learned carpentry at Potroso and later earned money by building benches and doors.

By the time the Potroso plantation closed in the 1930s, another avenue to earn cash to meet subsistence needs had become more available for men like the Blancos of Loma Bonita. Several large sugar plantations had been established in the lowlands of Coclé Province in the late nineteenth century, and some highland men had always made the long, tough foot journey to work there during the cane harvest. But this trickle of hires had become a larger stream by the 1930s, after construction of the gravel road through Coclé's Pacific lowlands (see Chapter 1) made the journey to the cane fields somewhat easier. Groups of six or seven highland men would travel down together by foot or horse to harvest cane for a short stint in June and July when their fields needed less attention. The group, I was told, would often employ a woman (sometimes the partner of one man in the group) as their cook, each man contributing to pay her a daily wage similar to theirs. Harvesting cane was hot, dirty, and difficult work – highlanders had to sleep on the ground in the cane fields – but they could earn 35¢ to 50¢ a day (less expenses for food, travel, and, often, alcohol and cigarettes). And, this money came at an auspicious time, during the "hungriest months" and during two important saints' days – San Juan (June 24) and Santiago (July 26) – when everyone wanted cash for liquor and special foods, like onions.

## ECONOMIC AND GENDER DIFFERENCES SOFTENED BY KINSHIP

When Esperanza was a child, her grandparents were among Loma Bonita's economically better-off families. This was because her grandfather, Natividad Ruiz, had inherited several hundred hectares of Loma Bonita lands and some cattle from his mother, Rosa, a daughter of Reina

Ruiz. Since Natividad was the only one of his siblings to make Loma Bonita his main residence as an adult, he could claim rights to much of it.

To be "better off" with land and cattle at that time meant to have a little more milk, cheese, and meat in your diet, and a few "luxuries" not available to everyone, like a metal roof or a new sugarcane press. It also meant that a family could occasionally pay with cash or meat to get agricultural help from others. And, importantly, it meant that a family could get the amount of extra cash required to meet subsistence needs without having to do the most exploitative types of wage work in places like Potroso and lowland sugarcane plantations.

But even the slight material edge that they held over others was ephemeral. At any given moment, this could change; my genealogies attest to the many people who suddenly died of disease, fell from a tree, got struck by lightning, or drowned crossing a river. Cattle, too, died frequently from falls and periodically from plagues. As Dionisio Ruiz told me, "When my parents became old, they had to support themselves by killing off most of their animals to eat or sell." When these problems arose, people needed to call on others from their wider kinship network for help. And, in Loma Bonita in the 1920s and early 30s, whether you were a Ruiz, Ortiz, or Blanco, you were kin – related somehow to Reina Ruiz – with certain responsibilities toward one another. Slight economic inequalities were always softened by supportive kin relationships.

In a similar vein, economic relationships between women and men seemed complementary rather than unequal. While I've heard stories about men who were controlling or violent with women (and occasionally the reverse), this was a time when women and men had equal rights to claim, work, and inherit both land and animals. It was a time, too, when both had significant and flexible roles in their family's agricultural work, and also could earn small amounts of cash selling their products (hats, ropes, baskets) or their agricultural labor for brief stints. As Esperanza once put it, "Men and women both had their important jobs to do; it took both to succeed."

~

Esperanza grew up as a poor highlander with one or two dresses, no shoes at all, and few material possessions. But this little girl was rich in relationships. "If I was in trouble," she told me, "I could show up at any house and get help. Everyone knew me; it didn't matter whether my parents were their good friends or not." That Loma Bonita's families exchanged all manner of assistance was key to survival. That they also had enough land and cash to meet basic subsistence needs – with little interference from political or religious outsiders – gave everyone a small measure of economic security and control over daily decisions about how to use their production, labor, and land.

Coffee and Copé were about to alter this way of life forever.

# 3

# Youth: I Could Always Quit and Go Home (1940s–1950s)

*Esperanza Ruiz spent her youth travelling between Loma Bonita and the transit zone where she'd work for short stints as a live-in domestic. A part of her earnings went to her parents in Loma Bonita to help them pay for necessities that their small landholdings could no longer supply, and to help them participate in the new world of coffee cash-cropping. Along the way, Esperanza experienced the exhilaration of learning novel things – and the indignities and exploitations of domestic work. Along the way, she searched for a good man to marry.*

*This was an early moment in the incorporation of Loma Bonita's production (coffee) and labor force into the national and global capitalist economy. In the process, some families benefitted more than others from coffee cash-cropping, and men gained more control than women over agriculture and community land.*

## 1939 – ESPERANZA'S ESCAPE

Esperanza's heart pounds as she lays in the dark, pretending to sleep. The only sound is the soft rhythmic breathing of her six younger siblings sleeping soundly side by side next to her in the kitchen loft. At first light, she'll need to spring into action. She reviews her plan, knowing that, if it fails, her parents will beat her. Quietly she'll sneak away from the others and climb down the wooden ladder to the kitchen where last night she hid an old flour sack. In the sack is her comb, a barrette, and three dresses – two hers, the other borrowed from her cousin Nivia. She'll put on the oldest dress, the blue one with white trim. Then, before anyone opens their eyes, she'll grab the sack and run away to the lowland town of Penonomé.

This plan has been brewing in her mind for a few days, ever since that man had raped her. No one knew. He said she couldn't tell, and she was afraid of him; when angry, he'd once hit a friend of hers so hard that her skin had welted up and left a nasty bruise. How could Esperanza get away from him? She'd leave and get work like her cousin Bianca had recently done. Bianca had spent six months in Panama City working with an aunt in the public market. When she came back, she had gained a little weight and her skin was lighter from not having been out in the sun all day. And she had new dresses, a pair of shoes, and a different hairdo.

Esperanza wanted all of this. She, too, would leave, get a job, buy new things, and be safe. She'd go to Penonomé where she knew a family who could help her. The son in this family had been Loma Bonita's teacher last year, and his mother, Sra. Paula, had sometimes come up to the community by horse to pick up and drop off his laundry. To Esperanza, they had seemed like kind people. But when she had told her mother that she wanted to go to Penonomé to work, Natalia had said, "No, daughter. We need the money, but you're my oldest, and I need you here to help with the children."

So Esperanza Ruiz, age 16, had hatched the sneak-away plan, telling only her cousin Nivia who had encouraged her to go there.

First light peeks into the kitchen loft, and Esperanza climbs quietly down the ladder, dresses, grabs her sack, and leaves her house behind. The 9- to 10-hour foot journey to Penonomé is tiring, but she knows the road; she's walked it a number of times with her mother. By the time she reaches the river, not far from Penonomé, she's famished. Not having brought any food in her sack to keep it light for her journey, she picks up a large stone, smashes the hard outer shell of the fruit of a tree (the courbaril), and eats the white part that covers the seed. It tastes good, but stinks, which is why she's never chosen to eat it before. But today, she's got to survive.

It's 2:30 in the afternoon when Esperanza reaches the narrow street in Penonomé where she and her mother had once visited Sra. Paula.

"Sra. Paula. Are you there?" she shouts.

Surprised but welcoming, Paula comes to the door.

"Hello, my child. Who are you with?"

"I'm alone and have come for your help to get a job, Sra. Paula. I know how to cook, and just need them to pay me something and give me food."

"Come in, sit down, and get something to eat, Esperanza."

While Esperanza is eating, Sra. Paula goes to the nearby home of a couple; the two have a bakery in their house and had recently told her they needed a domestic worker. They agree right away to hire Esperanza, starting tomorrow. For $5 a month, she's to work six days a week, from 7:00 a.m. to 7:00 p.m., cleaning the house, washing dishes, and sweeping and mopping floors. But no cooking. Sra. Paula offers Esperanza a small room in her house to sleep each night. No charge.

Esperanza works hard at her new job. She's thrilled about the food; every day her employers give her just-baked bread from their oven and an egg and coffee with milk. And to Esperanza Ruiz, her $5 salary is a lot of money.

A month slips by. With her first month's pay, Esperanza goes straight to a store to buy things for her family: a 100-pound sack of rice for $2.50, a large bag of bread for 20¢, and an ivory comb.

"It looks like you'll spend all your money without leaving any for yourself," says the store owner. "Would you like to buy a piece of material for a new dress?"

"Do I have enough money left?"

Yes she does, and Esperanza buys three yards of a lovely cloth with rose-colored flowers.

The next day, while sweeping outside she sees a young man from Loma Bonita and asks him to take a note to her mother to come with a horse to pick up her new purchases.

For four more months, Esperanza works for the Penonomé couple. Then, tired of working and content with her purchases, including her first pair of shoes, she quits and goes back home with the money she'd saved for her parents. Years later, she'll tell me that this was a good first job, that they, and Sra. Paula, treated her well.

Esperanza stayed in Loma Bonita for the next few months, helping her parents in the house and fields. But it turned into a time of deep grief. After eating a large number of mangos, her 15-year-old brother suddenly got terribly sick and died. "If it hadn't been such a sad time," Esperanza told me, "my cousins Felipa and Bianca and I would have been enjoying ourselves by going to *juntas*, drinking corn beer, and flirting. If there'd been a dance anywhere near Loma Bonita, we'd have walked there to meet boys. But no. My family was in mourning."

Then came January 15, 1940, the celebration of Santo Cristo in the lowland town of Antón. Esperanza's family traveled there every year and stayed with her mother's sister, Carlota, who had married one of Loma Bonita's first teachers and gone to live with him in Antón. Aunt Carlota had a proposal for Esperanza. Did she want to work for a woman Carlota knew in Panama City? With her mother's permission, Esperanza gave a resounding "yes." She was enthusiastic to earn money for clothes and shoes for the family, and to help her parents buy coffee seedlings.

Within days, Esperanza was in Panama City for the very first time. "It was exciting," she told me:

> There were so many things I'd never seen before, like washing machines, movies, big buildings. I learned how to cook with gas. Everything was new for me, because where I came from everything was pure *monte* and more *monte*.

But Esperanza hardly got to see the city. She worked endless hours at this job, six and a half days a week, for $12.50 a month. Even her half day off on Sundays wasn't all hers because she had to clean up after the family ate at noon. But in the few hours she did have, she and cousin Bianca would meet at the room of a woman they knew from back home where highlanders in the city often gathered on Sundays to share stories and have fun. Sometimes, they'd walk to the nearby ocean wall and peer over it at the moving seawater; occasionally, they'd go to a movie. But Esperanza wasn't happy. "After a year at that job,

I quit and went home," she told me. "I was tired of being treated like a slave. They wouldn't even pay my vacation."

It was 1940 when she returned to Loma Bonita with clothing for herself and her family, a cot, and money for her parents; she'd been sending up to half her salary home when she could.

> I was only 18 years old when I got back to Loma Bonita from that job, but I needed to rest. Too much work. I know there were washing machines [in the city] at the time, but where I worked you had to wash a ton of things by hand.

## THE LURE OF COFFEE

Back at home, things were tough for her parents, who by 1940 were short on land to meet all the basic needs of their other five still-young children. Her stepfather, Teodoro, had no land of his own in Loma Bonita, and her mother, Natalia, had only the plot she had gotten from Manuel Blanco when Esperanza was born, as well as the small amount of *monte* land her father, Natividad, allocated every few years. Thankfully, one of Teodoro's relatives had recently helped with a gift of about six hectares (almost 15 acres) that he didn't need in a place called Frailecito, about a two-hour walk away. On parts of this land they could grow food crops to supplement their Loma Bonita harvest. Unfortunately, though, it wasn't suitable for coffee.

Coffee cultivation had become the rage in Loma Bonita and the region, beginning back in the 1920s when several lowland merchants had moved up to tiny Copé. One, Felipe Meng, had opened a general store and offered to buy highlanders' products, especially coffee, to resell down in the lowlands. Never before had the people of Loma Bonita been able to earn cash for their products so close by. Everyone had wanted to plant coffee. (See Figures 3.1 and 3.2 for images of coffee production in Loma Bonita.) But not everyone could. A few families had fared better than others because they were able to access land in higher altitudes, best suited for coffee. Natalia's father, Natividad, had been one of the most successful back then. But by 1940, although elderly, he had not yet chosen to divide his estate among his children.

**Figure 3.1. Washing coffee beans at stream before drying, 2011.**

Natividad's decision to keep control of his lands was, of course, one reason his daughter Natalia was in such a tight economic situation, without enough land to provide a livelihood for her family. A similar dilemma confronted almost half of Loma Bonita's families by this time.[1] In part, these land shortages were simply the result of natural population growth, which had left each generation with a smaller land pie to be shared. In part, coffee cash-cropping had exacerbated this problem because Copé merchant, Felipe Meng, in alliance with Natividad Ruiz and another community man, had managed to lay claim to almost half of Loma Bonita's cultivable land, leaving less for the community's other families to claim and divide up.[2]

The question facing land-short households, like Natalia's, was this: what do you do if you need cash for your family to live but don't have the resources to join the "coffee craze"? Only one path came into view – wage work. World War II helped them out. In December 1941, the United States entered the war and virtually took over Panama with its canal, initiating activities, especially in urban areas, that created a flood of unskilled jobs in construction and services, jobs that paid three times prewar and rural wages.[3] Included among US war projects was the improvement and paving of the old gravel road along Coclé's Pacific

**Figure 3.2. Harvested coffee beans being dried on the ground in people's patios, 1980s.**

lowlands, and this new part of the Inter-American Highway made it easier for Loma Bonita's workers to get to the slew of new jobs.

## URBAN MIGRANT IN A TIME OF WAR

Esperanza had been in Loma Bonita for a year when the war broke out, helping her parents build a new one-room house in Frailecito. One Sunday, her cousin Bianca dropped by and raved about the great-paying jobs available in the city because of the war. Esperanza was immediately on board to go, and her mother, in need of money for the new house, agreed. Teodoro had recently left to look for work digging ditches near the capital, and Natalia had no idea if he'd bring anything back.

Esperanza quickly found jobs in the capital, first as a restaurant waitress and then at a hotel where she learned about prostitution in a time of war. As she told me,

> It was the kind of hotel where people rented a room to have sex. There were 17 rooms, and my job was to bring beer to the customers'

> rooms; I had a key to each room. The boss, I learned, had a special room with a hole in the wall to peer at the guests. I was making big money there with tips, but it ended when the police raided the hotel and sent many to jail. Luckily, the police found me sleeping in my room with the door open and let me go. I went right home with my new dental bridge, and money for Mama to buy a mare.

For a while, Esperanza stayed in Loma Bonita and got involved in a possible new "love interest," with a man named Jaime from a nearby community. They'd courted for a few months, but Esperanza had doubts about him. As she later told me,

> Jaime had a reputation as a womanizer. He'd gotten my cousin Felipa pregnant, but denied paternity. Then one day, I was washing clothes at the stream while Jaime was in the house with Mama. Mama told him that she didn't want her daughter to be with a man who wouldn't be responsible for his children. Jaime came down to the stream. He raised his machete and smashed it down hard on a boulder near where I was squatting. He told me what Mama had said, and ordered, "Pack up now and get ready to come home with me. But know I won't forget other women."

"I thought about it for a second," recalled Esperanza, "and then I said, 'Aha, thank you for the invitation, but, as the saying goes, to be forewarned is to be forearmed [*en guerra avisada, no muere soldado*]. Goodbye, go home.'"

## URBAN MIGRANT IN SEARCH OF A GOOD MAN

During World War II, almost a third of Loma Bonita's unmarried men left the community to work in urban areas,[4] mostly on construction jobs. But when the war ended in 1945, this work dried up and most men returned to Loma Bonita to tend to their family's food and coffee crops. Not so for the community's unmarried women, the vast majority of whom (80 percent), like Esperanza, had gone to work in the city at least once during the war. Panama's postwar economic boom only increased the urban demand for low-paid, live-in domestic workers to serve an expanding middle class. And Loma Bonita's parents who, like Natalia, lacked enough land to feed their growing families, continued to relinquish their unmarried daughters to fill these jobs in cities and towns.

Esperanza was among them. At a cousin's suggestion, she returned to Panama City to take a restaurant job and brought her 16-year-old cousin Katia with her. At the restaurant, Esperanza met a man she liked named Damien and, after a while, went to live with him in his rented room in the capital, bringing young Katia along. But Damien turned out to be another womanizer. Said Esperanza,

> For a long time, I was stupid. Damien got Katia pregnant, and I didn't know that he was the father. They kept it secret. Katia's mother in Loma Bonita said I should send Katia home. But I said no, I'd be responsible until she gave birth.

After the baby was born, Esperanza got Katia to safety with relatives, and decided to give Damien another chance.

> That's when Damien took me far away to live with his family near a rural town way past Penonomé. Truthfully, I had no idea where I was, and no money to get home. Damien's family treated me well, but he was bad. When he got mad, he'd bring other women to the house or hit me. His mother defended me and said, "If you don't love this woman, you should let her go." He would say, "This ruined woman will die in my arms." And I would tell him, "Yes I feel ruined for living with you."

Esperanza's mother, Natalia, told me how it ended:

> For a long time, I didn't know where my daughter was or how bad she was being treated. Finally, though, a man she knew in the town lent her money for her fare back here. My daughter asked for my help and promised not to go with Damien anymore.

~

**BOX 3.1 A WIDER LENS: COMMERCIAL COFFEE GROWING IN PANAMA, POST–WORLD WAR II**

In Panama's postwar booming economy – supported by US and foreign banks as well as by international moneylenders such as the World Bank and International Monetary Fund (IMF) – greater coffee production was one goal of the Panamanian government. This was a time of rising coffee prices on the global coffee market; the price for a pound in Coclé's lowlands rose from about 12.5¢ before the war to 25¢ in the early 1950s and 40¢ by the end of the decade. Coffee production in Coclé Province increased by two-thirds during the 1950s.[5]

Government programs that aimed to increase coffee production reached Loma Bonita's region for the first time in the 1950s. Government workers were sent into highland communities to teach people how to prevent coffee diseases, as well as to buy highlanders' coffee and sell them inexpensive seedlings (5¢ apiece) on easy credit. Many of Loma Bonita's farmers participated in these programs.

The year was 1949 when Esperanza left for the city once again to earn money to help her parents buy coffee seedlings and fencing for their small Loma Bonita landholding. Coffee had gotten even more profitable after the war.

This time Esperanza went to Colón City. Her cousin Marcela was living nearby with two young children and a man named Máximo, who was the father of her baby. On a visit to Marcela's one Sunday, Esperanza learned about her cousin's desperate situation. Máximo was treating her badly, Marcela said, and never gave her any money. To get clothes for herself and the children, she'd been buying flowers around her neighborhood and lugging them and the children into Colón City to sell. She pleaded with Esperanza to help her get away. Esperanza related what happened next:

> Our Aunt Elena was working in Colón, so I went to her house to ask what we should do. Aunt Elena had this idea: I'd buy a bottle

> of rum and take Máximo, Marcela, and the two children to the big dance on the weekend. We'd get Máximo drunk, and when he fell asleep, sneak away to the highway. In the meantime, Aunt Elena would go to Marcela's house, grab her clothing and five chickens, and bring them to the highway where she'd wait for us.

This plan wasn't easy to pull off, as Esperanza told me:

> At the dance, my heart pounded with fear. Finally, Aunt Elena's son arrived and whispered that everything was ready at the highway. About 3 a.m., when Máximo was passed out drunk, we snuck away and got a car to Antón and then Penonomé. From Penonomé, we had to walk the rest of the way home to Loma Bonita with tired children and agitated chickens. But we made it.

That wasn't quite the end of the story. About a week later, a letter from the government's municipal office arrived in Loma Bonita with a warrant for Esperanza to appear. She was charged with "breaking up a home." Máximo was at the hearing when Marcela, Esperanza, and Esperanza's mother, Natalia, arrived. Marcela told the magistrate that she had begged Esperanza to help her. Natalia testified about the bad conditions of Marcela's life. The magistrate dropped the charges.

After a few months in Loma Bonita, helping her mother and flirting with a young man named Andrés Blanco, Esperanza got a message from a cousin named Diana, beckoning her back to work in the capital. Esperanza didn't know this cousin well because, when young, Diana had been taken by a Loma Bonita teacher to live in Panama City where she had gone to school and eventually married. But Diana would become Esperanza's first urban anchor, providing her with a dependable place to land when Esperanza was looking for a job or fleeing bad urban times.

In the course of the next three years, with Diana's help, Esperanza held several live-in servant jobs – some good, some bad. Then, in 1953, she faced a monumental personal crisis and asked her employer for a week's vacation to return to Loma Bonita. She had missed one menstruation and thought she might be pregnant. In the past few years, on her vacations and holidays at home, she and Andrés Blanco had spent time

**BOX 3.2 A WIDER LENS: RURAL-URBAN MIGRATION IN PANAMA AND LATIN AMERICA, POST–WORLD WAR II**

The migration of rural youth to urban areas in search of paid work during and after World War II was not unique to Loma Bonita. In Panama during these years, population growth in the countryside and increased inequality in the control of land[6] left masses of poor farming families without enough land to provide their basic needs. Their main option was to send their children to labor in towns and cities to earn cash for necessities. One result was an urban explosion: the percentage of Panama's population living in urban areas jumped from one-third in 1940 to almost one-half in 1970.[7] In fact, by 1960, almost 40 percent of Panama City's population had initially migrated to the capital from the countryside.[8]

Other Latin American countries experienced similar urban developments in the post–World War II era, triggered also by rural population growth and increasing land inequality. Between 1940 and 1970, the number of people living in urban areas in Latin America jumped from one-fourth to one-half of the total population. And, as in Panama, since most rural-urban migrants moved to only one or two major cities in their countries, the number of cities housing half a million people in Latin America jumped from 8 in 1940 to 20 in 1960.[9]

together. She liked him. Andrés was a hard worker. And considerate. She knew that, unlike many men who drank and smoked their money away, Andrés, after working in the city during World War II, had returned home with a large cooking pot and clothing for his family – and a horse. She also knew that someday he'd inherit some good coffee land from his father in a nearby community and from his mother's small lot in Loma Bonita. She decided that, if she were pregnant, she'd want to live with Andrés. She told me,

> When I missed my period, I told Andrés right away. It's important to do this so a man can't later disclaim the baby. Andrés didn't believe it. I

> stayed in Loma Bonita all that month, waiting, but still no period. I told Andrés again. He said that, if I was pregnant, we could get together, but he didn't offer a plan of action. So, on July 28, I left to go back to work. Andrés lent me his horse to go to Penonomé, but didn't go with me.

On returning to work, however, Esperanza learned she had lost her job; because she was a few weeks late returning, her employer had replaced her. She made her way to the apartment of cousin Bianca's sister, María, who had just begun to live with a man from the capital. Right away, Esperanza found a job through a newspaper ad, but within months she was fired. Here's why.

> It was lunchtime on Sunday. I had made the family's meal and was getting ready to go to Diana's on my only half day off. But then my boss's daughter arrived with her husband and child, and my boss told me to make food for three more. I said, "No. This is my free afternoon." I told her that, although she might think I was an uneducated ***chola***, I wasn't anybody's slave. Remember, Gloria, I was quite pregnant, and got mad fast.

Esperanza left and showed up at cousin Diana's door, unemployed and six months pregnant. Andrés had not answered her letters, and she was considering Diana's offer to stay with her and have the baby in a hospital. But then came the urgent message from her mother. Esperanza's beloved grandmother, Benita, had died. Esperanza remembered that trip home. "When I got to Penonomé, my brother was waiting with a horse that Mama sent. The ride home was really hard because I had so much pain in my belly."

Esperanza spent the last few months of her pregnancy with her family in Frailecito and Loma Bonita. Then she had a fall and hurt her back. Andrés took her to a nearby healer who said she was too old to have the baby at home and should go to the hospital. "No way," said Esperanza. "Home is what I know."

At that time, Andrés was going back and forth between his house and hers but said nothing about living together. He had another woman in a community a few hours away and hadn't decided which one to choose.

It wasn't an easy birth. Esperanza recounted:

> For two days in Frailecito, I had pains but couldn't give birth. That's when my brother went to Loma Bonita to bring Andrés back to our house. He'd been on his way to visit the other woman, but he and his father came here instead.

Tony Blanco Ruiz, son of Esperanza Ruiz and Andrés Blanco, was born that day in March of 1954. Said Esperanza,

> Andrés told me I could come live with him and his family in Loma Bonita, that he would build another room onto the house for us. "No," I told him. "There are too many men in your house." At that time, there were five brothers and two nephews living in Andrés's grandparents' house. So I stayed in my mother's house in Frailecito, and Andrés came to live with us, though he went back and forth between our two families.

That same year, Esperanza and her mother used their combined savings to pay for a small coffee farm in Palmar, a four-hour climb from Loma Bonita. Andrés also planted coffee on his father's land. Finally, they had a toe in the world of coffee.

Esperanza and Andrés had some difficulties in the early years of their marriage. One day, for example, Esperanza caught him with another woman from a nearby community. According to Natalia, Esperanza was so furious that Natalia had to restrain her daughter from doing something bad to this other woman. Such experiences did not end Esperanza's union with Andrés, however, and in 1957, they built their own one-room house, with thatch walls and roof. Although their new home was only five minutes away from Natalia's house in Frailecito, Natalia cried when they left.

Esperanza and Andrés were married in 1959 in a free mass-marriage ceremony in the Catholic church in Copé. Three of their children were with them. Two more would soon be born. "Why did you decide to get married?" I asked Esperanza years later. "To live in the grace of God."

**Figure 3.3. Esperanza and Andrés, together 50 years later, 2007.**

## ESPERANZA'S PREMARRIAGE URBAN CAREER

During Esperanza's 15-year urban career before marriage, she held 11 jobs, mostly as a low-paid, live-in domestic worker in the capital. Trapped in the confines of her employers' homes, she had little power to negotiate better working conditions. But she did hold one great big card. As Esperanza put it, "I could always get another job in the city, and I could always quit and go home." In fact, she quit six of her eleven jobs between 1939 and 1953 because she had been poorly treated, sexually harassed, or assaulted. This action of self-defense and defiance was possible because her parents in the highlands still had enough land to support her returns to Loma Bonita. The same held true for most of Loma Bonita's young, unmarried women migrants at that time. Subjected to previously unknown forms of labor exploitation, classism, racism, and sexual abuse in the urban world, most, like Esperanza, considered urban jobs as temporary affairs, necessary to earn cash in order eventually to return to the highlands to marry and raise families at "home."[10] Surely, though, they didn't return home unchanged. Along with their unprecedented exposure to discrimination and abuse, they brought home a wealth of new learning about the big wide world, a touch of independence, and some control over the small but desired cash rewards of their labor.

## MOTHER NATALIA'S FIGHT FOR LAND IN A MAN'S WORLD

The money that Esperanza and later her sisters sent their mother from their urban salaries did help relieve Natalia's economic problems in Loma Bonita, paying for food, clothing, chickens, school supplies, household goods, housing materials, coffee seedlings, and even a horse. At the same time, however, their frequent and long absences from Loma Bonita when they were employed in the city worked against their mother when she tried to defend her land rights against men in her family and the government.[11]

It was a February morning, about 1950. Natalia had decided she would plant that year on a plot near her old house site in Loma Bonita, a piece of land that her father, Natividad, had designated for her before he died. She hadn't worked that land since moving her main house site from Loma Bonita to Frailecito a decade ago.

Natalia organized a *junta* to help her work her fields because only one teenaged son was living at home. Her three daughters, including Esperanza, were in the city working, and her husband, Teodoro, was gone, living somewhere on the Atlantic coast near two of their sons. Years before, Teodoro had so mistreated her and their children that Natalia had kicked him out. "Better off alone than with a man who's trouble," she had told me, her lower jaw protruding out as far as it could go. "I told him, 'You have a choice: leave here as a free man or go to jail.'"

On the February morning in question, Natalia was awaiting her *junta* workers when her brother Dionisio showed up. He was furious. She had no right to use this land, he said. It was his land, he said, since he was the one taking care of their elderly mother. "No," she yelled back. "Papa Natividad gave me this piece of land to work for my family." But Dionisio insisted she leave.

Natalia Ruiz had reached her limit. She and her six children needed land to grow food, and Dionisio already had most of their father's land.

"I was really, really mad," Natalia told me. "So mad that I was ready to go to the magistrate's office to file a lawsuit to get my rightful inheritance."

She sent a message to Esperanza and her other two daughters in the city to come home to accompany her and bring money for a bribe for the officials. None could leave her job right away, and the sisters could scrape together only $10 on such short notice. So Natalia went alone to the magistrate's office, no money in hand. When she arrived, Dionisio was already there, and presumably he had made his case with the authorities. Unlike Natalia, he knew the officials in this office, as Dionisio, like his father before him, had been Loma Bonita's *regidor* in the past. After a brief exchange of information, the magistrate told Natalia, "Go home. When you and all of your siblings are together and agree to settle your land claims, send word to us, and we'll arrange a meeting to discuss partitioning the land."

Dionisio returned home very angry with Natalia and took it out on their elderly mother, Benita, scolding her for not telling Natalia to drop the case. In tears, Benita called Natalia to her side and begged her to drop the idea.

Natalia felt cornered and alone without her daughters to accompany and defend her. Nor could she get her sisters living nearby to help. Two were ill, and all had daughters who were also away working in the city. Besides, they were sure that Dionisio would win because of his influence with the magistrate. And he had a proven violent streak, which made them afraid for their mother and themselves. Natalia decided she had to let it go, "to leave it in God's hands." She didn't want to watch her mother suffer.

The meeting to partition the estate of Natividad Ruiz never took place. I did not get Dionisio's side of this story, and he died in 2001. But, in fact, he emerged in control of most of his father's land and animals, despite the national law granting male and female children equal rights to the parents' inheritance.

Natalia did end up with about eight hectares (almost 20 acres) of land in Loma Bonita, a small part from her father's estate and the rest land given to her by Manuel Blanco at Esperanza's birth. These landholdings, along with what she and Teodoro had been gifted in Frailecito, helped make it possible for her children, including Esperanza, to raise their own families in Loma Bonita. But the next generation, Natalia's grandchildren, would grow up in a different world.

## COFFEE CASH-CROPPING, MIGRATION, AND EMERGING GENDER INEQUALITIES

Natalia was not alone in her battle or defeat; I know of several other community families in the postwar years that had similar land dramas, which ended with similar results for the women.

Coffee cash-cropping and urban migration together were tipping the scale in men's favor, undermining the more gender-equitable agricultural economy of Esperanza's childhood when women and men seem to have equally asserted their rights to claim, inherit, and work the land (Chapter 2).

How did coffee cash-cropping become a culprit in this emerging gender inequality? It brought outside "power holders" – men like merchant Meng and government officials – more directly into Loma Bonita's community affairs. Being men themselves and operating in the context of a male-controlled national political economy, these merchants and politicians, not surprisingly, made alliances and business deals mainly with highland men, like Natividad and Dionisio Ruiz. One result – male victories in land disputes.

Urban migrations played right into these male economic advantages in Loma Bonita. With all three of Natalia's daughters working far away in the city, for example, Natalia wasn't able to muster the quick cash and political support she felt could help her win her land rights. Migrations also gave Loma Bonita's men an edge over women in agricultural production. With young women, like Esperanza, moving frequently back and forth between the community and urban places, they were no longer as regularly available as were their fathers and brothers to work in the family's fields. On top of this, their frequent absences left the other women in their households – grandmothers, mothers, and sisters – with more childcare and household work to do, and less time for agriculture.

This decline in women's access to family lands and in their contributions to agricultural work was happening slowly. Women still were claiming and inheriting some of their families' estates, just not as much as men. They still were working in their families' *montes* and coffee farms, just not as regularly as men. And, at the same time, it was their urban labor and spirit of kinship that was making all the difference to the welfare of their families.

# Adult: A Voice Meant to Be Heard (1960s–1980s)

*As mother and wife in a young family without enough land for subsistence, Esperanza returned to doing short-term domestic work in the city. Years later, when her children also left to work there, she guided them through the dangers and pleasures of urban life. As an adult community member in Loma Bonita, Esperanza was an outspoken force, using her energy and faith to work cooperatively with others on government and church projects that she hoped would relieve everyone's economic woes.*

*This was life during two decades of military rule in Panama that kept hope and fear taking turns. In Loma Bonita, coffee (and orange) cash-cropping increased with government encouragement, but so did population growth and, therefore, land shortages. A need for cash pushed a second generation of young people, like Esperanza's children, into low-paid jobs in Panama's transit zone. Unlike their parents, most would not have enough land in Loma Bonita to be able to return to the highlands to raise their own families.*

## 1967 – A GOOD HOUSE BEFORE I DIE

This is an ordinary Friday in June of 1967, but something unusual will happen in Esperanza's family before the day's end. It's 6 a.m. in Frailecito, and the rooster marks the hour with his boisterous call. Five-year-old David and two-year-old Sophia are in the kitchen eating breakfast with their mother. Their father stacks wood for the stove nearby. The three older children, Tony, Viviana, and Lety, have already fetched water from the stream, eaten their rice and coffee breakfast, and put on school clothing. Esperanza comes to braid Viviana's hair, and Andrés, Lety's. The children leave the house reluctantly because it's raining and they face a walk that can take two hours. No student in Loma Bonita's school lives farther away.

Parts of the path are pure mud and slippery. Still, they try to walk swiftly. At the stream called "The Dogs" – the most dangerous of the three streams they have to cross – 13-year-old Tony grabs the hands of his two younger sisters. They arrive late, wet, and muddy, but the teacher pays no attention, and the day passes without incident.

The way back from school is fun, even though it's still drizzling. Tony, Viviana, and Lety each walk with friends; all are in search of mangos and other beloved fruits to eat. On a low-lying branch of a tree, Viviana spots a bird's nest with three featherless babies. She captures two before the mother returns; tonight, her parents will roast them to eat with yuca or rice. When the children reach the stream of "The Dogs," they see him. The dirt on his khaki-colored shirt tells them he's just come from his *monte.* "Papa," they scream and run to him. Andrés is waiting to help them cross the stream in the rain. All three children love walking with their father. He's always in good spirits, rarely angry. Just by lowering his voice, he can get them to be good. Their mother … that's a different story. They love her, but she's big on scolding and sometimes uses a leather strap and hits hard. On those days, the children have heard their father calmly tell her, "To children we give food, not the strap."

Back home, the rain has stopped, and the children take off their good outfits and hang them up to dry. "Lunch is ready," yells Esperanza from the kitchen, a one-room structure with walls and roof made from sugarcane leaves that shield the waist-high woodstove. Under the mango tree outside the kitchen, the family crowds around a small wooden table made by Andrés. Esperanza serves Andrés first, a big bowl of soup made with bananas, yams, and yuca, and another bowl of beans. Then she serves the children. Andrés's bowl is quickly emptied. "Would you like more soup?" asks Esperanza.

"Yes, I'd like more," says her husband, hesitating a long second before adding, "than before." This familiar joke gets everyone laughing.

After lunch Andrés prepares to return to his *monte*. "Who, besides Tony, wants to come help me?" he asks. "Me, me, me," both older girls shout, since they'd rather work in the fields than fetch water and wood, sweep the patio, husk coffee, or practice hat weaving. Besides, their father often gives them permission to bathe and fish in the nearby stream, favorite afternoon activities. Esperanza decides. "Viviana, go with your father. Lety, stay here to help me."

It's not until dinner that Esperanza and Andrés break the news. Esperanza speaks.

> Children, I'll be leaving on Sunday to work in Panama [City] for a while. I don't want to leave you, but my cousin Diana has found me a job so we can get money to fix up this house. I want a good house for you before I die, one with adobe walls and a strong metal roof, and with real beds instead of those banana trunks and cowhides up in the loft. While I'm gone, I want Lety to sleep with baby Sophia. Papa and Grandmother Natalia will take good care of you. And soon we'll have that new house.

This news makes Lety feel happy thinking about all the food and clothing her mother will bring back. Viviana feels sad that her mother will leave but relieved that she won't have to face Esperanza's occasional wrath. All five children are content to stay with their father.

On Sunday, Esperanza, Andrés, and their five children walk down to Copé; Tony carries baby Sophia on his back. Quite a crowd has gathered near the church because people can now get a car there to go directly to lowland towns and the capital. Last year, the government finished a 26-kilometer (16-mile) paved road from the lowland highway up to Copé as part of a drive to promote commercial agriculture in this region. They want highlanders to grow and sell oranges as well as coffee, and this road makes it possible for buyers to get trucks up to Copé and, during the dry season, to Loma Bonita and beyond. For Andrés and Esperanza, the days of those 8- to 10-hour foot treks to Penonomé to catch a car for the city are over, that is, as long as they can muster the $2.50 fare.

Esperanza climbs into the passenger car. Andrés and the children climb back home. But first, as always, Andrés buys each one a treat: today, a lollipop. Joy.

It's not just the new house that's pushing Esperanza to the city to work again. She and Andrés have been having a difficult time raising their young family without enough land to meet their basic needs. At first, they thought that selling coffee would give them enough cash to buy necessities, and they both planted trees on their land. But just when these coffee trees began to produce in the early 1960s, the price of coffee on the global market dropped, and Copé's merchants reduced the price paid per pound from 40¢ to 35¢. Meanwhile, the cost of items in Copé's stores was rising fast.

So coffee, it seemed, couldn't save them. And getting more land for food from their families' estates was out, too. On Esperanza's side, her mother, Natalia, had six adult children with whom to share her small landholdings. And Andrés was one of seven grown siblings who would soon be dividing their parents' land.

They'd tried one other way to get more land for food crops in the early 1960s, but it almost crippled Andrés. At the invitation of Esperanza's cousin Marcela, they'd packed up their belongings and children and made the grueling, seven-hour foot journey through mud and rain across the Continental Divide to the "other [Atlantic] side." It was a wild, beautiful area where people were few and fertile public lands abundant for "use." Marcela had claimed use rights in the government's district office to a large lot of land there.

Esperanza and Andrés planted and reaped bountiful harvests of rice, corn, beans, and yuca on "the other side," but life, said Andrés, was very, very hard.

> There were no roads, doctors, stores, or schools – pure snakes, insects, and dangers. Marcela's nearest neighbor was a half-hour walk away. If a child got sick, you had to carry them back to Penonomé. Some died.

Then, Andrés suffered a serious knee injury, and the family had to return to Frailecito and Loma Bonita to live year-round. This is why Esperanza had decided in 1967 that there was no other way to build their new house than to leave for the city again to earn money as a domestic.

**BOX 4.1 A WIDER LENS: US IMPERIALISM AND PANAMANIAN SOVEREIGNTY, THE EARLY 1960s**

When Esperanza journeyed from Copé to Panama City on the new paved road in 1967, she had heard rumors that the United States had paid for this road. She could not have known, however, that the road was part of a larger US effort in the 1950s and early 60s to counter what it viewed as the threat of rising left nationalism in Latin America. On the one hand, the United States sent its military troops into certain countries (Guatemala, Dominican Republic, Cuba) to help overthrow their "undesirable leftist" leaders. On the other hand, the US government sought to create a buffer against leftist movements by giving "preferred" governments enormous sums of economic assistance to support reforms for the poor and middle classes. Through the Alliance for Progress and Peace Corps, created in 1961, the United States supported infrastructural development (like Copé's road) and other rural projects.[1]

The Panamanian government was one recipient. Between 1961 and 1963, it got $41 million a year in US economic assistance, six times the annual average provided during the 1950s.[2] All this money, however, could not stem the tide of nationalism in Panama where the US-controlled canal and Canal Zone and the presence of US military forces had fed resentful popular protests throughout the twentieth century.

Then came January 9, 1964. That day, US high school students in the Canal Zone raised the US flag at their school, in defiance of an order by the Zone's governor. Word spread, and about 200 Panamanian students – angry about the absence of the Panamanian flag and about the disrespect for their country's sovereignty – marched into the Zone and tried to raise their own flag at the school. Hostile US Zonian adults joined the Zonian students and surrounded the Panamanians. In the scuffle that ensued, the Panamanian flag was torn, and things turned violent. Rocks were thrown, and before long the Canal Zone police were using tear gas and guns. The crowds on both sides got larger and angrier, and the US army, stationed nearby, was called in. Thousands of Panamanians, hearing about the flag desecration, joined the "rebellion for sovereignty," and the fighting spread within the capital and to other parts of Panama. Panamanian and US militaries halted the rioting a few days later, but anger at the United States seethed: 22 young Panamanians (and 4 US military men) were dead, and hundreds were injured. Panama broke diplomatic relations with the United States for a few months, but eventually this rebellion would lead to negotiations between the two governments to eliminate the Canal Zone and return the canal to Panama. January 9 is commemorated each year in Panama as the "Day of the Martyrs."

In the course of the next few years, Esperanza would hold seven urban jobs, each for a few months. She'd leave two jobs because her bosses didn't pay her, another three when she felt badly treated, and two more because Andrés sent word that he needed her at home. With her earnings of $25 to $30 a month, Esperanza would send $10 to Andrés for food, save $10 or $15 for the new house, and use the few remaining dollars for her own expenses. "It was so sad missing my children," she later told me.

> Sophia was only two when I first left. The worst part would be when I'd serve a good meal, and my boss would tell me to throw out the leftovers. Good food, delicious. I would think of my baby eating boiled yuca at home, and cry.

By the late 1960s, Esperanza had saved enough money to finish the new house. Her daughter, Sophia, later reminisced, "For us, this one-room house was beautiful, because it was new. We even had real beds that Papa made. We were content. We didn't know about other [fancier] houses, so we were happy with what we had."

Once again, Esperanza was an unknowing pioneer, one of the first married women of her generation to leave husband and children in Loma Bonita and go work in the city. Some people disapproved. As she told me,

> They said I was walking the streets (of Panama City) looking for men. But I didn't care; people just like to talk. My mother helped Andrés with the children, until people even "talked" about them. So Andrés started doing everything himself, *monte*, house, children. He's always been that kind of man. His father was, too. Many men aren't.

## 1960s – LAND INEQUALITY AND URBAN MIGRATION

Esperanza and Andrés were far from alone in their economic dilemmas. By the mid-1960s, population growth and family land divisions had left about 75 percent of Loma Bonita's families without enough land to meet most subsistence needs.[3] Like Esperanza and Andrés, these land-poorer families had come to depend on paid work to survive. They were sending more of their able-bodied men to harvest cane in the brutally hot sugarcane plantations in Coclé's lowlands[4] and many more unmarried members (plus a few married women) to labor in low-paying jobs in urban Panama. By this time, almost 75 percent of the community's unmarried females (aged 12–50) and about 20 percent of males in this age category had migrated at least once to work in a city or town.[5] Community women still worked almost exclusively as live-in domestics; men usually worked as gardeners, supermarket baggers, or construction workers.

In contrast, most children, especially males from the community's few better-off families with adequate landholdings, could avoid the most exploitative jobs of migratory wage labor in cities and plantations. For example, by 1970, Esperanza's uncle Dionisio Ruiz had 13 children with his wife, Belsi Ortiz. None of their six grown sons had ever migrated to work in an urban area or (with one brief exception) a lowland plantation. Instead, some were sent to school to learn about agriculture, car driving, or mechanics.

## 1968 – A FRIDAY THAT CHANGED PANAMANIAN HISTORY

October 11, 1968. On that Friday in Panama City, the country's National Guard staged a near bloodless, successful overthrow of the country's newly elected civilian president, Arnulfo Arias. By this time, Panama's traditional oligarchy had proven itself unable to make necessary economic reforms or win control of the Canal Zone, and its members were deeply divided over whether to continue the ISI economic policy. Into this breach of power, stepped Panama's National Guard.[6]

The leader of the new military government was Colonel (soon-to-be Brigadier General) Omar Torrijos, son of a teacher in a small rural city. With his newly granted official title as "Supreme Leader of the Panamanian Revolution," Torrijos shut down Panama's previous legislature

### BOX 4.2 A WIDER LENS: IMPORT SUBSTITUTION INDUSTRIALIZATION (ISI) IN PANAMA AND LATIN AMERICA, 1960s

On the surface, Panama's economy in the 1960s seemed to be thriving. In addition to its traditional emphasis on agricultural exports and international services in the transit zone, the country had been industrializing since the 1950s;[7] by the 60s, it had one of the highest average annual economic growth rates in Latin America.[8]

As in much of Latin America since World War II, Panama had based its industrialization on a strategy referred to as ISI (import substitution industrialization), a development model promoted by US and foreign banks and by international moneylenders, like the World Bank and International Monetary Fund (IMF). The ISI strategy called for the creation of industries within each country to produce for domestic consumption goods that previously had been imported. By the 1960s, however, it had become clear that the ISI development model was not generating enough jobs to improve the lives of most people; industries tended to be small, and those owned by US citizens or other foreigners imported from their home countries everything from machines to managers and used advanced technology requiring few laborers. In fact, by the 1960s, international moneylenders considered ISI to have been a failure in most Latin American countries and were instead promoting a different development strategy: export-led industrialization.

In Panama in the early 1960s, ISI had brought great wealth to a small segment of Panama's business elite and to foreign investors – and had increased the middle class – but almost half the labor force in the poorer sections of Panama City was unemployed or underemployed.[9] By the middle of the decade, unemployment in the country reached 25 percent, and in rural areas, per capita yearly income was estimated at less than $44. Panama's workers, students, and unemployed were in the streets protesting these conditions throughout the decade.[10]

and stripped its traditional oligarchy of political (but not necessarily economic) power. This was going to be a different Panama.

General Torrijos led a three-pronged project of change for the country. First, in line with shifting policies of the US and international moneylenders, he turned away from the ISI economic model and moved instead to expand greatly Panama's historic role in international commercial and financial services in the transit zone. This included creating an offshore banking center, a transisthmian oil pipeline, and a modernized duty-free and tax-free area called the Colón Free Zone, all of which would integrate Panama more thoroughly into the global economy. Second, Torrijos promised a new treaty with the United States that would end US domination of both the canal and the country. "We will stand or die, but we will never go down on our knees," was one of his famous slogans challenging US imperialism.[11]

Finally, Torrijos pledged to improve conditions for the majority of Panama's poor and working classes. For poor farmers in the interior, where about half the population still lived, his new initiatives involved land reform, economic and social development projects, and expanded political participation. Incorporating poor women into this fray was a stated goal, and posters everywhere read, "Women will fight with you, Omar – now and always." To administer this large-scale effort, the Torrijos government set up new army posts all over the countryside where military men took on the double role of policemen and community development workers tasked with initiating cooperatives and health and school projects. One post was established in Copé; another in a community that was a few hours' climb from Loma Bonita.

## 1972 – TORRIJOS'S REFORMS: WHEN HOPE AND FEAR TAKE TURNS

On this April morning in 1972, three months since my arrival in Loma Bonita, I awake to the soft clucking sound of tiny geckos on the ceilings and walls of Francisco and Tina's two-room house. Next comes Tina's cheerful morning greeting. She returned two days ago from her three-month job at the Catholic school in Panama City, and had seemed relieved yesterday when Esperanza (at my request) offered to continue providing my meals.

After my morning rituals, I leave for Andrés and Esperanza's house for breakfast. Eleven-year-old David is crying when I arrive, his big black eyes and long lashes drenched. Esperanza is instructing him, "Don't cry, son. Everything dies. We'll bury him soon." It turns out that David had tied up their small horse in the pasture last night but found the horse dead this morning. Strangled by the rope.

David calms down and takes a seat at the small wooden table between his big brother, Tony, and younger sister, Sophia; Esperanza, Andrés, and I sit crowded on the other side of the table. That's when I learn that 18-year-old Tony – a young man full of warmth and playfulness – will be leaving next month to work in Panama City for the first time; his two sisters, Viviana and Lety, left for the capital last year to work as domestics. Tony tells me he'll live with Esperanza's cousin Diana and work in a restaurant. He's excited to go.

Another family decision surfaces at this meal: Esperanza and Andrés plan to move their main residence from Frailecito to Loma Bonita year-round to make it easier for the children to get to school and for the whole family to get to Copé's stores and transportation.

After breakfast, David and Sophia leave for school, and Andrés and Tony depart for their *monte.* Luckily, Esperanza's cousin has lent them 3 hectares (7.4 acres) to plant food crops this year, a gift of "kinship and friendship," Andrés told me, with no need to return anything.

Esperanza and I are alone, seated on two low wooden benches in the patio. I seize the moment to talk about her new "starring role" in the election project that Sergeant Vito Delgado first announced at a big political meeting in Copé last month.

Sgt. Delgado is one of the military men that the Torrijos government sent to this area in 1970 to set up an army post a few hours' climb from Loma Bonita and to initiate "community development" projects in the region. At the meeting in Copé, Delgado had told people that in August, voters in each municipality would choose someone to represent them directly in a brand new national "Assembly of Municipal Representatives" that would meet periodically in the capital. "This is one way," Delgado had said, "that my commander and chief, General Omar Torrijos, wants to help you."

In the wake of that announcement in Copé, Loma Bonita's *regidor,* Sr. Cristo, had called a meeting at Loma Bonita's school to help Delgado, his political ally, get the "New Panama" election project started. My fieldnotes record the meeting's events.

> Sr. Cristo told people they had to elect two new committees – one for men, the other for women. Committees would then collect funds for the "New Panama" election project by sponsoring raffles and dances. Without further explanation, Cristo opened nominations for the women's committee. A long, embarrassing silence. No volunteers. Someone called out Juana Duarte's name. "All in favor?" asked Sr. Cristo. A few called out "yes." Without further ado, Juana was "elected" to the committee. The same painful process was repeated again and again, until most posts for the two committees were filled. Among the many people who didn't volunteer but were "elected," like Juana, were Esperanza and Andrés, the new presidents of the women and men's committees.

Esperanza had sought out Sr. Cristo after the meeting. "I'm confused," she said. "I don't understand why we're supposed to raise money or why women and men are separate." Sr. Cristo had explained that the goal of committees was to back the Torrijos government by raising funds for the candidates. Since women are especially good at raising money, he said, the government wants separate women's committees. "But what if you're not for this government?" Esperanza had asked. "Then we'll know who you are," was his ominous reply.

Climbing home after that meeting – out of earshot of Sr. Cristo – people had spoken their minds. Most in this group had initially opposed Torrijos because he had deposed President Arnulfo Arias, their political hero. One man in the group now said that he thought Sr. Cristo had become Delgado's (and Torrijos's) spy in Loma Bonita. Others agreed. Andrés aired other frustrations. "They've now put me on four different committees, each with meetings, raffles, and dances. When am I supposed to find time to burn my *monte* to get it ready to plant when the rains come?" Then Esperanza spoke up, in a voice meant to be heard:

> Here's what I see. We'd better carry out this committee work, whether we like it or not. Look, Delgado and the other army

> men here walk around in their military uniforms and guns, and probably talk directly with General Torrijos in Panama City about everything we say and do.

No one disagreed. Fear was palpable.

~

That meeting in Loma Bonita's school was a few weeks ago. Today I want to talk with Esperanza about what has happened since. Several people, she says, have informed Sr. Cristo that they want to quit their committee posts. Before she can finish this story, we hear a voice calling from the patio. "Good morning." It's Juana Duarte, Esperanza's niece and member of the women's committee. Juana is my age and so shy that she often lowers her eyes and hides her mouth behind her hands when she speaks. She lives nearby with her husband and his parents.

Juana confides in Esperanza that her mother-in-law and husband are angry about her work for the women's committee and are accusing her of going to meetings "to look for men." Her mother-in-law even told Juana to quit or leave the house – but without her children.

Esperanza tries to comfort Juana and spur her on.

> I can't tell you what to do, Juana, but your mother-in-law is wrong. You're doing important work for the women's committee. When we started this committee work, I was confused and scared about this government and Delgado, with his gun and his way of going after all the young girls. But I've started to think in a different way.
>
> What if this "New Panama" election is our chance to vote for someone – not from Copé or below, as always before – but from up here near Loma Bonita? Someone who could tell General Torrijos and his people in Panama City about our real situation. Maybe this government will be different and listen to what we need.

Esperanza goes on to tell Juana about her new idea: to get Sr. Cristo of Loma Bonita elected in August as municipal representative. "Andrés and I are in agreement," she says. "We want Sr. Cristo and are ready to work for him in our committees."

Juana sits quietly listening as Esperanza encourages her to try to smooth things out with her family and stay on the committee. "We have to cooperate together to try to improve our life here, even if we're afraid," Esperanza tells her.

She sends Juana home with an armful of plantains, and then she tells me that she feels sad for Juana and grateful that Andrés never stops her from doing what she wants to do. "But men are divided on this," she says, "and I've seen that even Andrés doesn't defend us women when he's with the other men. Anyway, I don't care what people say about me. Let them talk."

It's 9:30 a.m. I get up to leave, but no … another visitor calls from the patio entrance. It's the vice president of the women's committee. She's come to ask Esperanza's advice about another committee member who won the lottery and abandoned her post to go work in Panama City. Should she report this woman's desertion to Sr. Delgado or Sr. Cristo? As I walk away, I hear Esperanza saying, "No, no, don't get her in trouble with them."

I walk back to my other home with Francisco and Tina to collect my notebook and camera. Tina is in the kitchen weaving her next hat. Francisco, as usual, is sitting in the front patio listening to the news on his blue plastic radio. I've noticed that neither Francisco nor Tina has attended political committee meetings in the last few weeks, but I've not felt comfortable raising the sensitive subject of politics. I sit on a bench beside Francisco, and this man of few words surprises me by starting a conversation about the "New Panama" election campaign. He says,

> They [the military government] only want our money. Prices are up, and, if we want to buy or kill a pig or cow now, we have to get permission or pay. If you talk against them, they take you to Copé to pay a fine. It wasn't like this before, when they didn't live so close. The most important thing we want here is a paved road! Ask anyone. When I see that road, that's when I'll cooperate with these committees and this government.

## 1972 – ESPERANZA AS MIGRANT MANAGER

It's already hot, humid, and sunny at 8:30 on this Sunday morning in September when it should, instead, be pouring rain. The drought this year has wreaked havoc on crops and people. I'm on my way to pick up Esperanza and Tina in my white Volkswagen camper, the car I had shipped from Pittsburgh to Panama last January at the beginning of my fieldwork. I keep it stored at a friend's house near Penonomé. I pull the camper up to the dusty bus stop at the crossroads of the Pacific lowland highway and the road to Copé. Five minutes later, the minibus arrives here from Copé, and Esperanza and Tina emerge looking scrubbed and fancy in their best blue and green cotton dresses and black plastic shoes. Esperanza's hair is carefully braided beneath her clean straw hat. Tina leaves her short, curly hair hatless. We're off to Panama City.

I'm going there for 10 days to work in the national land archives and interview migrants from Loma Bonita. Tina and Esperanza were the only community members who could come along for the free ride this time. We three are feeling lighthearted to be together for this urban adventure. Tina laughs as she tells us she has only 75¢ to her name but that her sister in Panama will help her out with money and a job at the Catholic school where she worked before. Francisco isn't pleased about this trip, she says, but they're broke; there's no money in Loma Bonita to hire him to build houses or furniture, the only things he loves to do.

I already know that Esperanza has come to check on her three employed children. Viviana and Lety have worked as domestics in Panama City for the past year, but recently they wrote to say they're unhappy and want her to find them different jobs. Tony left for the city for the first time a few months ago and works at a restaurant, but Esperanza hasn't heard from him since he moved out of cousin Diana's house and rented a room with two of his cousins.

Esperanza also has a second mission during this trip: to ask the three children for extra financial help to buy a small plot of land near their house. Last week, Sr. Cristo had offered them this lot for $61, a good price because it has 98 coffee trees and 4 orange trees already producing. Since Cristo won the election for municipal representative in August, he's needed cash to pay his travel to meetings, his meals in the capital, and for nicer clothing. Esperanza and Andrés thought it was sad that he had to sell land to get money, but they were thrilled for a chance to add to their small landholdings. Andrés even had a dream about it, "a great dream that I bought this land from Uncle Cristo, and it had just been weeded and was beautiful." Esperanza had explained to me, "This land is for the children, so they'll have something later. It's not for us, we're already old."

"Do you think he'd have offered you the sale if you hadn't supported him in the election for representative?" I'd asked her. With a shrug and a grin, she said, "Maybe not. And I've been thinking that, after he's sworn in on October 11, I'll ask him if he can get better jobs for my children in Panama."

~

We've been on the road to Panama City for only a short time when Tina begins to sing a song that she's "invented" about a woman who falls in love. Her voice is strong and melodic. Esperanza and I join in. Then, as often happens, our conversation drifts to the subject of sex, pregnancy, and contraceptives. Esperanza talks about her fear that her daughters in the city will get pregnant, and maybe not get good men. She's warned them by mentioning a long list of young women from Loma Bonita whose lives are much harder because they got pregnant by a man from the city who then left them high and dry. Esperanza adds,

> Contraceptives, they're a problem, too. The thing doctors put inside you [an IUD] people say causes cancer, and the pills and operation are way too expensive. These doctors don't know anything about the difficulties of our lives.

She never went to see a doctor, she says, until she was six months pregnant with David at almost 40 – it was too expensive.

> What if they tell you that you need medicines or hospitalization? How embarrassing to not be able to pay. And what if you die in the hospital, but your family doesn't have the money to bring you home for burial? Which is what happened to Andrés's mother. No, if I'm going to die, I'll die at home so my family doesn't have expenses.

This leads to the subject of local healers, the main medical practitioners used by highlanders. Esperanza and Tina each describe the many miraculous cures they've experienced and seen.

After several hours of talk and banter, we enter Panama City's snarled traffic jams, and I drop Tina off at her sister's workplace in a Catholic high school. Esperanza and I go to visit Tony in the restaurant. An exceptionally short man with shifty eyes greets us and says that Tony was fired a week ago. With zero consideration for Esperanza's feelings, he tells her that Tony was stealing food to give to two of his "bad cousins." Esperanza apologizes profusely to him in a low voice I've never heard before. We leave. "How embarrassing," she says, a few tears trickling for the first time since I've known her. "Oh my God, what will we do for money?" is her first thought. The second, "We have to find Tony."

We make the rounds. He's not in the room where he lives, one of a long row of rooms lining an oblong building in a slum area of the city. Crammed into the room that he shares with the two other young men, I see three cots, a radio, a small wooden table, a few benches, and clothing hanging every which way on an overhead wire. Close by, facing the line of rooms, are a few communal outhouses and showers and several large cement basins with faucets for washing.

We drive next to the apartment where his sister Lety works for a former teacher in Loma Bonita, and while we're there, Tony shows up with sister Viviana; he's gotten word that we're in pursuit of him. Tony looks handsome in a new Panama shirt, shiny black shoes, and with a gold (looking) watch on his wrist. Viviana is quiet; she has Esperanza's heavyset body and dark, expressive eyes. Tony's version of what happened puts the blame on a girl he worked with at the restaurant. He tells Esperanza that he's been looking for another job.

Esperanza listens but says nothing more about the situation. She and I, and her three children, bid farewell to Lety's employers and climb into my car. Next stop, another dilapidated section of the city to visit Andrés's two younger brothers who live in a room similar to Tony's. I leave Esperanza's children off near the entrance while she and I go to find parking. We walk back on a street packed with people talking, yelling, laughing, singing, fighting, and often sipping beer. I see two young women whom I know from Loma Bonita strolling toward us and am excited to stop and chat. But they pass us, with a cool "hello," and move on.

"What just happened?" I ask Esperanza. "They acted as though they didn't know us. Was it because I'm with you?"

"No, Gloria, it's me. In the city, those two girls, and others – sometimes my own children – are embarrassed by me. I know what they're thinking: 'Here comes the *chola*.'"

I take a closer look at Esperanza. Well, yes, she's clearly a poor woman from the countryside. She has on a clean dress, but it's blousy, not modern. Her black plastic shoes, braided hair down her back, and, above all, woven straw hat mark her rural, poor status.

We spend the rest of that day visiting relatives and end up at her cousin María's house. That night, after Tony and his sisters leave, Esperanza agonizes over what to do. Should she let Tony stay in the capital and earn money to send home? Everyone at María's has an opinion. By the next morning, Esperanza decides that Tony's not ready yet. Tomorrow they'll catch the bus home.

~

I stay in the city another week to visit Loma Bonita migrants. First on my list is Esperanza's 14-year-old daughter Lety. I've only met her a few times, and we don't yet have a comfortable relationship. I'm not sure what to expect. She opens the door to her employer's small two-bedroom apartment in a lower middle-class neighborhood of the city and welcomes me with her only available arm; the other holds a baby, and there's a toddler at her feet. Lety is skinny, with shoulder-length hair and dark eyes. Her family calls her "*Negra*" (Black) because her skin is darker. Her employers are away, so we can speak freely.

I ask how she got this first job.

> When I finished [primary] school, Viviana [her older sister] had already left to work. I didn't want to be left behind to be a slave, and I wanted to continue school to learn how to sew. So when someone in the community told Mama that Loma Bonita's teacher was looking for a domestic in Penonomé, I was enthusiastic to leave. I was happy to be working, but right away also sad because I missed my family a lot. I'd think about them all the time. Papa wrote to me, and I read and reread his letters.

In addition to cleaning the apartment, Lety takes care of two babies and washes and irons their clothing. (Years later she'd tell me, "I arrived still a child, to take care of other children.") She likes to sing and play with the children, she says, but the very best part is getting paid.

> The first time I went shopping with my employer I bought something for David and Sophia, and, for myself, some pretty gold rings, a watch, and shoes.

"But why do you want to leave the job now?" I ask. Lety mentions a few things she doesn't like, including that she has to sleep in the living room and can't go to bed until her two bosses finish watching television there. But more important, she says, is school.

> My boss won't let me go to school because she says she's going to the university at night. But actually, she doesn't go to classes. I told Mama that I think she just doesn't want people like us advancing, not even a little.

And there's another pressing reason that Lety wants a different job; the teacher's husband keeps sneaking up to where she sleeps on the sofa and touching her. She stood up to him once, she tells me, and even told his wife, but she needs to get away from this abuse.

When I leave Lety, I feel as though I've gotten to know her a little. I love her spunk and am moved by the ambition and forthrightness of this 14-year-old girl.

During the next 10 days, I visit and speak with 11 other migrants from Loma Bonita. Some visits go well, and I learn a good deal about their lives. Others are less successful, with embarrassment as thick as peanut butter.

A few days later, I return to Loma Bonita with Tina who has scored big and is in high spirits. She's earned $7.50 by working for seven days: two with her sister at the Catholic school and five in the home of one of the school's teachers. In addition to cash, she lugs two big cartons of food and a hefty, oversized sack of used clothing from the teacher. Yet part of the story she tells me is a heartbreaker. The mother superior at the school, she says, treats her like garbage, criticizing everything she does. And she found out through her sister that the mother superior had forewarned the teachers against hiring her, saying, "Tina is too ignorant. She never finished first grade, and doesn't even know how to read." As Tina relays this to me, it's clear that she resents the treatment. At the same time, she keeps me in stiches with her impersonation of the "too ignorant mother superior."

Back in Loma Bonita, after 10 days of the hot, noisy city, I arrive at Esperanza and Andrés's quiet home for dinner. Right away I ask Esperanza about Lety's request for help getting another job. Esperanza has already gone to talk with a teacher in a community a few hours climb away, requesting that the teacher take Lety in and help her learn to sew. Esperanza told the teacher she'd deliver Lety to her "as though she's your own daughter." But, Esperanza tells me, "If this doesn't work out, I'll go back to Panama myself to work so Lety can leave her bad job."

Enter Andrés and Tony, back from their *monte*. Tony carries a big basket of harvested corn on his back. After dinner, I ask Andrés if he'd been angry about Tony's return. "To the contrary," he responds,

> I have so much work here to do, but there's no one around to help, even for pay. I'll soon be 50, and all I've seen is work. The young men now go to the city or the plantations to earn money. And young women, they're all in the city; they're not even around here for the young men to marry. Tony's a great worker, and I need him.

Tony smiles in agreement. I ask him how it felt to leave the city. "Sad. But I'll get back soon."

**BOX 4.3 A WIDER LENS: THE DEMISE OF TORRIJOS'S SOCIOECONOMIC REFORMS, 1970s**

Hope and fear dominated the political landscape in Panama throughout General Torrijos's military government of the 1970s. While the proliferation of government programs to promote economic and social development and to expand political participation generated hope, it didn't take long for global events to unravel most of these projects. In 1973, OPEC raised oil prices and the Western world economy descended into recession.[12] In Panama, this meant less demand for Panama's services and goods, which was especially serious because Torrijos's policies had emphasized expansion of international services and export production. Panama plunged into economic decline; in 1976, its economic growth rate ground to a halt,[13] and funds for Torrijos's reform projects for the poor were diverted elsewhere. By the early 1980s, some new schools, health projects, and roads had been completed, but the country suffered high unemployment, falling real wages, and soaring inflation and prices.[14] Panama by then had the highest rate of income inequality in Central America; 40 percent of the rural population and 12 percent of urban people did not have sufficient food.[15]

These global and national changes played out in Loma Bonita. During my yearlong presence in 1972, the community became a beehive for government development projects, including the "New Panama" election campaign that I've discussed. Within a few years, however, these efforts fizzled or died as global and national pressures redirected funding and attention. Their demise was due also to the top-down and undemocratic way government representatives, like Delgado in Loma Bonita, implemented this work, as illustrated by the experience of Esperanza and others in the "New Panama" election.[16]

We'll never know how Torrijos might have dealt with these problems. On July 31, 1981, he and six others boarded a plane in Penonomé for a short ride to a community just over the mountaintop from Loma Bonita. The plane crashed. All aboard perished. (Some consider this crash suspicious because two other key opponents of US policy in Latin America, President Roldós of Ecuador and General Hoyos of Peru, died in similar accidents within months.) In one indisputable way, Torrijos changed Panama forever. In 1977, he and US President Jimmy Carter signed the Torrijos-Carter treaty that dissolved the US Canal Zone and set a timetable to transfer full control of the canal to Panama on December 31, 1999.

## 1984 – CATHOLIC PRACTICE AS SALVE IN HARD TIMES

I'm back in Panama again and headed for Loma Bonita, my 10-year-old son Reid by my side. This is the first time Reid is accompanying me for my whole field trip although five years ago he and his father had visited me in Loma Bonita for a few days. At 6 a.m., we climb into the car going from Panama City to Copé, and as soon as we arrive, I spot Heraldo Vásquez getting out of a shiny, red truck. He's the owner of a small store in Loma Bonita and now, he says, of this truck. He'll take us up to the community for a *peso* (50¢) each, "and a cigarette," he adds coyly. He looks disappointed when I tell him I stopped smoking four years ago.

Along with 13 other people and their cargo, Reid and I climb into the open back of Heraldo's truck and sit packed like sardines on benches that line both sides. Up we go. This is my first time up by car rather than on foot, and I'm exhilarated to be moving through familiar space with such unfamiliar force and speed. I'm also terrified. Like everyone else, I'm holding on for dear life to anything solid, while clutching my son, as the truck dodges giant stones and deep gullies. Since 1972, this road has been widened and leveled a bit, but the long-promised paved road never materialized. When we reach our destination 20 minutes later, I pay Heraldo $1.00 and, with enormous relief, step onto firm ground.

There's a new, small store at the side of the road, and Victoriano Ortiz shouts a big hello from behind its front counter. After exchanging greetings, Reid and I set off on the narrow path lined with coffee and orange trees that leads to Tina and Francisco's house. Behind us trails the noisy squeak of Heraldo's truck straining to continue its climb on the red-brown muddy road snaking up the steep mountainside. Ahead, our surprise.

I've told no one that we would arrive today. I'm already imagining Tina's laughter at first sight, but it turns out she's in the city taking care of her sick mother, and Francisco has gone to Penonomé to buy supplies. We continue on to surprise Esperanza and Andrés.

"*Oiy, Oiy,*" I call out at the entrance to their patio, noticing that their two-room house, with adobe walls and metal roof, has finally been finished. Right away, I see her sitting on a wooden stool on the edge of the patio, a book in her lap, a pair of too large, black-rimmed glasses covering much of her face. For a moment, Esperanza looks startled, but she quickly places glasses and book (a Bible) on the ground and comes running, arms open, mimicking my call, "*Oiy, Oiy.*" Andrés is right behind her. Embraces all around. Esperanza turns to me, eyes damp, as are mine. "You've come back, and brought your son."

Andrés carries four wooden benches to the area outside the kitchen, which is still a one-room, thatched-roof structure, now with two walls made from metal sheets tied to wood posts. Esperanza immediately lights the woodstove to make us coffee. She no longer has to climb down to the stream to get water. Instead, she walks to a spigot set up in the patio near the kitchen. Loma Bonita's system of plastic pipes carrying

**Figure 4.1. First meeting of Catholics in Loma Bonita to elect Delegates of the Word, 1979.**

water to people's homes is an improvement made during the Torrijos years; the government provided some pipes, but community members had to raise funds for the rest, and donate much labor. "Let's see if the spigot wants to give me water today," jokes Esperanza as she launches into examples of times the pipes have broken down when she was in the shower covered with soap. Today it works.

Andrés and Esperanza are now 61 years old, and Andrés's black hair is full of white flecks. He's as bone thin as ever; Esperanza's equally stout. I ask about their children. "We're alone," says Andrés, "Tony, Lety, and Sophia are working in the city, Viviana and her two children are living far away in Darién with her husband, and David is in Penonomé continuing his religious studies, God willing, to be a priest."

David a priest. I've been following his religious path since my field visit in 1979 when he was elected at a prayer session of Catholics in Loma Bonita to be one of the community's first "Delegates of the Word" (see Figure 4.1). Delegates are lay leaders, trained to bring community members together to talk about Catholicism and their lives. Every few months after his election, David – along with about 60 similarly elected young men from other poor, rural communities in the province – had attended a four-day, church-led seminar in Penonomé. They studied

**BOX 4.4 A WIDER LENS: THE CATHOLIC CHURCH AND DELEGATES OF THE WORD, 1980s**

After the Vatican II meetings of the Catholic Church in the 1960s, a movement swept across Latin America aimed at revitalizing Catholicism while helping the region's masses of poor. Referred to as liberation theology and the Christian-based community (CEB) movement (in Panama, "Delegates of the Word"), this religious and social initiative inspired progressive Catholic clerics, often defying the "established church," to locate lay leaders in poor communities and teach them how to organize discussions in their own communities about the Bible and the struggle to improve life. One of the earliest CEBs was established in Panama in 1963,[17] and during the 1970s and 1980s, others were slowly organized around the country.[18]

religion, the church's position on socioeconomic issues, and methods for carrying out their work. Between seminars, he and another delegate had spent half their waking hours in Loma Bonita organizing a dizzying array of activities, including a religious committee, weekly prayer sessions, Sunday "celebrations," and the construction of a chapel.

Clearly proud of her son, Esperanza brings me up to date while Andrés whisks Reid away to check on the chickens and recently captured turtle.

> When David finished his four years of training to be a Delegate of the Word, he was one of about 30 young men who Father Henry invited to continue on to secondary school and religious classes in Penonomé. If David succeeds, he could go on to study to be a priest. A sacrifice, but, if God is willing, a beautiful one.

"Who pays his expenses?" I ask. "The church pays for the seminars and classes," Esperanza reports, "but not for transportation, food, and notebooks."

> David has earned a little by working in the cane fields during school vacations, but we've all helped. There are special costs, too. When David needed an algebra book, Sophia offered $14 of her salary. Before that, with her very first paycheck in the city, she bought

> her brother a Bible. Last year, David mentioned his desire for a typewriter. Tony found one for $80 in the city, and Andrés went to pick it up. Thanks to God and our children, and to our oranges too, he's still studying.

That's the family's good news.

Next I learn about pressing problems. "With all our children gone," Esperanza laments, "there's no one here to help us in the fields. I keep trying to convince Tony to come back with Noris (his wife) and their children, but she won't come."

Andrés and Reid return, and I get to ask Andrés about this year's harvest. He's proven to be one of my most accurate teachers about agricultural matters.

> Ay, Gloria, this was a bad year. The winds in February were so strong that we lost most of our oranges, and our coffee has been dying from diseases for years. Our last good coffee harvest was in 1974, with about 400 pounds. Now, in a good year our trees give maybe 50, and, in a bad year, like 1980, only 35. It's this way for most people here, except families living higher up on the slopes.

Andrés is a man who lives, breathes, and dreams about his *monte* and crops, but not long ago, he tells me, he was unable to work the land properly:

> My knees and legs got so bad that I could hardly walk. Viviana had to come from the city with her children to help Esperanza harvest, and Tony came to take me to the capital where he and Lety dragged me to doctors. All those doctors did was take our money. Gone was our hope of buying a horse for $40, or those $80 glasses for me. We didn't even have money for all the medicines they prescribed. For two years, I could only work here near the house.

Slowly, however, with the help of a healer near Loma Bonita, Andrés's knees have improved enough for him to plant corn and beans in Frailecito this year.

Reid and I devour the coffee and bun of soft white bread from Copé that Esperanza serves, while she apologizes for not having "better food."

**BOX 4.5 A WIDER LENS: THE 1980s – THE DEBT TRAP AND NEOLIBERAL REFORMS IN LATIN AMERICA AND PANAMA**

Most countries in Latin America in the 1980s faced their worst economic crisis of the century. Encouraged in the past by US and other foreign banks and international moneylenders to borrow heavily, they now were unable repay. Banks responded with a "debt trap": they allowed governments to reschedule loan payments and borrow more money, but only if they agreed to a series of demands referred to as "neoliberal economic reforms and structural adjustment austerity programs." These "reforms" especially hurt poor and working people, for example, by reducing or eliminating public spending on government employment and health and education services. Everywhere, massive unemployment and growing poverty were the result. Everywhere unprecedented numbers of people responded with collective actions of resistance against the impacts of neoliberal reforms.

Panama was no exception: by the early 1980s, it had the highest per capita foreign debt in Latin America, in large part, a result of loans received in the 1970s to pay for Torrijos's programs. Torrijos's successor, General Manuel Noriega, continued to take out new loans, pulling the country deeper into the banks' debt trap. By the mid-1980s, official unemployment in Panama reached 12 percent,[19] and its citizens were in the streets again and again[20] protesting neoliberal economic policies.

Andrés explains. "Times are hard with General Noriega's military all around us and prices for everything going up," he says. He's referring to the less charismatic and more corrupt general who took command of Panama's military after Torrijos's death. Andrés continues:

> Things are so bad in the capital that our children often can't help us out. Tony and Sophia both lost jobs for a while last year, and Viviana and her whole family gave up and left to live far away in Darién [a province in eastern Panama] where the government is giving poor farmers lots of land to use to plant food crops. I hope to go there this year and bring back corn for the house.

"In this dark time of Noriega, thank God for our church," Esperanza adds in a cheerier tone. Then she stands up to announce that we must all leave right away to get to Nella's house in time for her Family Assembly (neighborhood prayer group).

In Nella's patio, the prayer group has gathered. I count eight people already seated who live in this section of Loma Bonita. Twenty-three-year-old Antonio Ortiz, one of Loma Bonita's current delegates, opens the meeting strumming a lively church song on his guitar. Everyone sings along. Then he tells a story about a peasant family whose seventh child dies of parasites. "Why do you think the child had parasites?" he asks. "Because the family is too poor to have safe water," responds Esperanza. The conversation continues about poverty and its impacts, with most people contributing something. Then Antonio asks if people think anything can be done about poverty. He guides the discussion to the notion of "unity" – that people in a community must help one another. "Faith, yes, that's important," he says, "but faith without action, no." Another lively song is led by Antonio, and the meeting ends, about an hour from its start.

Everyone stands and moves from person to person, touching hands in greeting. There's a warm and friendly atmosphere in this patio, a sense of *alegria* (joy). Nella tells me that these meetings make her feel less alone now that her children are leaving to work in the city. And, she says, she feels freer to speak out here about "this terrible time of General Noriega." Andrés adds that when he works on projects for Delegates of the Word, he feels so tranquil that he doesn't want to stop.

Later, after dinner at Esperanza's, conversation ambles back to the ways the Delegates of the Word movement is trying to "put faith with action into practice." Last year, delegates started a cooperative labor exchange group to address everyone's labor and cash shortages, an attempt to revive the idea of *juntas*, which had almost disappeared with the growth of wage labor migration. The idea was that members would give a certain number of days a week to help each other in their fields. "We joined right away," says Andrés.

> Things started out great. But now there are problems: some members have received, but not given back, and others have had to leave to work in the cane fields. Two families have already dropped out. I don't know if this group will last.

"Now Delegates [of the Word] are talking about starting a food coop," Esperanza adds. She's not very optimistic:

> I'll join, because I like cooperative things, but I still remember what happened to the last one we worked so hard to organize during Torrijos. How our store manager "ate up" all the merchandise, and we lost the money we invested. Maybe with God's help, this one will turn out better.

Andrés says he's not yet sure he'll join.

After dinner, Andrés gets up to wash the dishes, and Reid follows him, eager to help. Once Esperanza and I are alone together, she goes right to the personal. "Noriega has made things even worse for us than before. We're all eating less chicken and eggs and more yuca, and sometimes skipping lunch or making soups instead of dry meals. The struggle is long." Still, her faith provides hope, and she continues in a lighter tone:

> But no matter how much it costs, I'm happy that David's in the church here. Near us. Not in the city. I try every way I can to keep him here. When he earned money working in the plantations, I encouraged him to buy a nice shirt instead of giving us all the money. And for breakfast, I try to give him an egg with his yuca. I want him to feel that he doesn't have to go to the city to be modern. I pray every day that we can help him, and God will see him through.

## 1980s – MIGRANT CHILDREN IN THE DARK DAYS OF NORIEGA

When Viviana was a little girl, her family called her "young Esperanza" because she so closely resembled her mother. She was 13 years old in 1969 when she finished primary school and, with her parents' permission, left Loma Bonita to work as a domestic in Penonomé, helping with housework and a three-month-old baby. A year later, this employer arranged for her to go to Panama City to work for a family friend.

Viviana was scared, never having been to the city, but slowly she adapted to the life of a live-in domestic in the capital, a life mostly of work under the watchful eye of an employer. In one crucial way, her urban life differed from her mother's early experience: Viviana had many other young relatives and friends also working and living in the city, and these soon came to include her three siblings.

That is how she met Bernardo Vega in 1975. On a Sunday at the bus terminal in Panama City, where many rural migrants hung out on their only day off, he was there with her brother. Viviana and Bernardo courted, and, despite her mother's admonitions, she was soon pregnant. But Bernardo had another woman and couldn't decide.

Before the baby was born, Viviana spent her month of vacation in Loma Bonita with her parents. What Esperanza wished was that her daughter would stay in Loma Bonita until the baby was old enough, and then leave the child with her and Andrés and go work in the city. "With only one child," Esperanza later told me, "Viviana could work and send money here to take good care of the baby. She doesn't need that man." But things turned out differently. Viviana's employer offered to arrange for Viviana to give birth in a city hospital and recover afterwards in her house. Viviana accepted the chance to get better medical care, also hoping that Bernardo would choose her.

But he was still indecisive three months after baby Isabel was born. So Viviana and Isabel moved in with her brother Tony, who lived in a large rented room with four others: his wife, Noris, their two children, and sister Lety. They had electricity and water in their room but shared two outhouses and showers with people from 19 other rooms in the building. Viviana found a domestic job right away with an employer who didn't mind her bringing Isabel to work when other childcare arrangements failed.

Viviana and Bernardo did finally get together when she was pregnant with their second child, and they moved into a rented room near Tony's. Their son, Sebastián, was born in September of 1977. With two babies to care for, Viviana's struggle escalated. Bernardo was working in a supermarket while she stayed home with the children and took care of neighbors' children to earn money. By the end of the year, however, she gave in to her parents' desires and her own needs and brought Isabel and Sebastián to live in Loma Bonita for a while so she could go back to work fulltime as a domestic day worker and save money for better housing.

When I visited Viviana two years later, in 1979, she and Bernardo were living in the same room with their two children. Also living there was her sister Lety who helped with childcare and attended sewing classes at night. Making ends meet was a major challenge for Viviana and Bernardo; room, food, and bus fare alone ate up almost half their salaries. Esperanza kept offering her home in Loma Bonita to the family or children, but Bernardo was adamantly opposed. He wanted the children to know and love him, he said.

Things between Viviana and Bernardo were turbulent. One Sunday, Viviana's siblings and Bernardo's mother were visiting at the house, enjoying cookies, cokes, and beer. Bernardo arrived home drunk and angry. In front of everyone, he grabbed Viviana's sweater and ripped it, and then fled. Months later when Sophia related this story to her mother, Esperanza's response was "Tell Viviana that next time she should hit him back."

When I again visited the family in 1981, Bernardo was still working in the supermarket and Viviana as a domestic. But they had improved their living situation. Along with tens of thousands of other low-income migrants, she and Bernardo had paid a $10 deposit to a government official and been assigned a small lot high up on an ultra-steep hillside on the outskirts of Panama City. For the moment, they had free rent in this government "urbanization project." On their lot, they had built a one-room house with wood-slat walls, a metal roof, and an earth floor. Soon thereafter, Esperanza and Andrés had come from Loma Bonita and brought yuca, beans, papaya, and plantains to plant in the small patio outside the house, as well as a few chickens to get them started. Viviana planted red hibiscus and other flowers for beauty.

Viviana was proud of her first home, and of their progress. Yet, as she pointed out, there was still much to do. The house was sweltering during the hot, humid day and damp and cold when the rains came. I've been there when rain converted the entire neighborhood into one vast mudslide and streams of water ran under Viviana's door leaving a muddy mess and swarming mosquitoes. Unable to afford electricity, they learned how to tap illegally into outside wires to power a bulb, TV, and small refrigerator, but candles, kerosene lanterns, and flashlights were still required. Outside was a tall metal drum to collect rainwater and, next to this, a rigged-up shower where everyone bathed quickly to evade the stinging ants marching in lines everywhere. Outhouses on these crowded slopes were so near one another that, as Esperanza always complained, the stench was terrible when breezes blew in certain directions. Her children retorted, "We've gotten used to it."

Then, in 1982, Bernardo lost his job. Given Panama's stagnant economy, he and Viviana, as I've noted, decided to follow his mother and sisters to a distant, unpopulated area in the forest of Darién Province that was being touted by the national government as a place of plentiful land to claim for "use."

Just to get there was expensive and arduous. For $6 each, they took a five-hour car ride from Panama City to the small town of El Tirao in Darién, a horrible trip on a road lined with gigantic potholes. Then came a two-hour foot journey on flat but incredibly muddy terrain, crossing the Sabanas River by stepping along a tree trunk, felled to serve as a bridge.

But they made it – with both children. After staying with Bernardo's family awhile, they built their own thatched-roof house with wood walls and an earth floor. The nearby river was their only source of water for drinking, cooking, and bathing. Life there, Viviana later said, was "like stepping back into my childhood when my family moved to 'the other side.'" The only school in the region was in faraway Tirao, and school was what mattered for her children's future. So Viviana took Isabel and Sebastián to live with their grandparents, Esperanza and Andrés, and attend Loma Bonita's school for the year. But she wasn't happy about this. As she told me, "I don't consider this an acceptable arrangement because children don't learn enough in Loma Bonita, and this could hold them back later."

About a year later, with a new son, Alexander, in her arms, Viviana learned a family secret that changed her life. Bernardo's sister let it slip: Bernardo had raped a woman she knew. When Viviana confronted Bernardo, and he denied it, she decided that she and her three children would have to leave him, and, knowing him, she realized this meant they'd have to "escape." After one failed attempt to get to Panama City, she confided in a man she knew who "had a truck and believed in justice." He got them safely to her brother Tony's one-room house, and from there, Viviana went to live with sister Lety and her young daughter.

Viviana lost all her possessions in the course of her flight, but she survived with her family's help and earned money for food and her children's schooling by helping Tony's wife Noris with her food business, taking in washing, selling sweetened ice to neighbors, and taking care of the children of her siblings and neighbors.

She and Bernardo spoke only occasionally after she left him. Until one crazy day. Viviana and Lety were at work that day, and Esperanza was at the house, having come from Loma Bonita to help take care of the children. Suddenly, Bernardo walked into the house, picked up his son Alexander, and left. Esperanza had no idea what to do. Viviana did. After work, she went straight to where Bernardo was living. He told her that he wanted the baby, but she could have the other two children. "My children are not little chickens that can be divided up," she told him. Actually, Viviana had previously prepared for this moment. Last year, she had met with a government official to ask if Bernardo had any right to the children. None, she was told, since he wasn't helping out at all. If he were to take the children, the official had said, she should come back to the office right away. Knowing this, Viviana threatened Bernardo, "Give me that baby, or tomorrow I go to the government official to report you."

"Take your son, but I'll give you nothing to help. Nothing."

She never asked anything more of him.

About the breakup between Viviana and Bernardo, Andrés told me, "If Viviana decided to leave, she had her good reasons." Esperanza said, "Good riddance. This man was bad to my daughter. And he never talked with me or gave me anything, not even transportation money when I visited."

## 1988 – ESPERANZA'S DASHED HOPES

Panama is in a deep economic and political crisis by 1988 due to the US decision to indict General Manuel Noriega for drug trafficking and launch an all-out war to oust him from power. In the process of cutting off all military and economic aid, the United States has destroyed Panama's economy, leaving as much as half the labor force unemployed.[21]

In Loma Bonita, Andrés is alone, stretching his food supply by eating less rice and more soup. Esperanza is in the city for a few weeks, taking care of children and grandchildren. David is mostly in Penonomé, having just earned a scholarship for six years of university-level study for the priesthood.

In the city, Tony, Lety, Viviana, and Sophia – with their growing families – are managing to survive this crisis economy, but with huge

**BOX 4.6 A WIDER LENS: 1989 – THE US INVASION OF MANUEL NORIEGA'S PANAMA**

It was 12:46 a.m. on December 20, 1989, when US President George H.W. Bush violated the Panama Canal treaties and international law[22] and gave the order to begin the invasion of Panama. In pitch dark, with no forewarning, the first bomb detonated.[23] In the next 13 hours, there were 442 explosions, just around Panama City. To capture one man, Manuel Noriega, the United States employed about 26,000 soldiers and stealth bombers. They killed between several hundred and several thousand (mostly poor) Panamanians (and 27 US citizens), wounded thousands more, and left 15,000 homeless. The US military called it "Operation Just Cause."[24] Some analysts maintain that the real reason behind this bloody war against Noriega was not drug related but rather that the United States aimed to replace him and his army with leaders more willing to comply with US policy in Central America.[25] Not until 2018 was this invasion officially condemned by the Inter-American Commission on Human Rights, which ruled the United States responsible for multiple human rights violations.[26]

struggle. Jobs come and go as employers lay them off for shorter or longer times. No one, however, says they want to go back to live in Loma Bonita in the foreseeable future. No matter how hard things are in the city, they tell me, there's a chance there to earn some money, and most important of all, the city offers far better schools. Their lives revolve around their children's education.

One day in late afternoon, Esperanza and I sit on wooden chairs in the tiny patio outside Lety's two-room house, surrounded in every direction by similar houses under construction. Esperanza is being critical of her whole family.

> My grandchildren don't listen. They just want to play, and their parents don't like me to hit them or yell. And my children, all they do is buy things that they couldn't bring to Loma Bonita, things that need electricity, like TVs and refrigerators. Do you know what my

> children tell their children when they won't study? "If you don't study, I'll send you to Loma Bonita to farm with your grandfather." Loma Bonita is like a punishment.

That night I write in my fieldnotes: "I think Esperanza is struggling to come to terms with this fact of life: neither her children nor her grandchildren will be coming back to live with her and Andrés in Loma Bonita."

# 5

# Elder: Doors Open, Doors Close (1990s–2019)

*As family and community elder, Esperanza has continued to be a woman on the move between Loma Bonita and the city. Now, though, she journeys not to serve strangers but to help her children and grandchildren negotiate life as urban citizens struggling to survive and improve their lot. Esperanza has faced accomplishments and tragedies wrapped protectively in her Catholicism.*

*This is life during a time when the global economy and culture intrude directly into Loma Bonita, bringing more commerce and outside visitors but still no easy path out of poverty. And this is when some of Loma Bonita's land enters the national and global capitalist market, becoming property as well as "home" – the property of wealthier lowland buyers. In the process, the price of land skyrockets, creating new divisions and conflicts in the community.*

## 1995 – SON DAVID'S TRIUMPH

Two years ago, at age 71, Esperanza told me she had changed her mind about death.

> When Sophia turned 15 [in 1979], I said to God. "Good, I've lived to see all my children grown, and now I can die." But, Gloria, look. Today Sophia is almost 30, and I'm still here. So now my dream is to live to see David graduate to be a priest. My son, a priest.

Now, two years later, she and I are discussing that dream. We're sitting in the shared patio between the houses of Viviana and Lety in an urbanization project named **El Mirador** that's perched high up on a hill in the outskirts of Panama City. Tomorrow, January 21, 1995, six young men from poor, rural communities in Coclé Province will be ordained as Catholic priests. David Blanco Ruiz is one.

Esperanza's daughters moved to El Mirador together, right after the US invasion of Panama in December 1989. Back then, the place lacked paths, streets, transportation, water, and electricity. Along with neighbors, Viviana and Lety organized activities to make improvements, clearing their own lots for houses they would build cement block by cement block (see Figure 5.1). Today, Lety's two-room house has a metal roof and earth floors. Most of her modest income from her seamstress job goes to school expenses for her 13-year-old daughter, and to help her parents and brother David in the countryside. Viviana's three-bedroom, cement-block house, where she lives with her four children, is more finished – with cement floors and glass windows. Although her salary as a domestic worker is smaller than Lety's, she gets financial help from her boyfriend of five years, an older man who is married but whom Viviana says treats her (and his wife and children) well.

"How are you feeling about tomorrow's ordination?" I ask.

"Nervous," says Esperanza. For the past three days she's been taking a Valium pill so that she can be "tranquil and happy, but not cry."

> Everyone who knows me says what a great achievement it is to have a son studying for the priesthood. People who don't know me see David in Loma Bonita and admire him and think his mother must be someone important. When they see it's only me, I like to tell them this saying: "from out of the old stump, comes the flower."

We reminisce about the 16-year journey that David and the whole family has traveled to get to this moment. I say, "I remember the day back in 1979 when he was selected to be Loma Bonita's first Delegate [of the Word]. That was the beginning."

"Yes," says Esperanza, "it's been a long, long road." She recalls the time when David was a Delegate, and they had no money to help him. "Then a miracle happened. A man arrived at the house and bought $15 worth of oranges, and we could send David $10."

**Figure 5.1. Urbanization project, Panama City, building a house little by little, block by block, 1990.**

I want to tell Esperanza that I've calculated that, over the past 16 years, she and Andrés have managed to contribute more than $2,000 toward David's education, not including the food they delivered weekly for years or the money and gifts from his siblings or the 10-year loss of his labor to the family. But I say nothing about this. Today is for celebrating, not analyzing.

Viviana emerges from the kitchen with a wet, warm cloth for Esperanza's nose, and scolds us for sitting under an avocado tree that only partially shades us. When I was here two years ago, Esperanza had been nursing a sore on the side of her nose that wouldn't heal. Viviana had taken her to a doctor who diagnosed it as cancer, but when he mentioned an operation, neither Viviana nor her siblings had insurance to cover their mother's health costs. Besides, Esperanza had said "no." No, she would never let anyone cut her.

But David had saved his mother. Esperanza had described how.

> When David was in Panama City last year, he met a nurse named Mariela who had grown up in Penonomé. She'd never been to a place

**BOX 5.1 A WIDER LENS: THE 1990s – INEQUALITY, CIVILIAN STYLE**

While bombs fell on Panama City the night of the US invasion of 1989, the urban children of Esperanza and Andrés gathered with neighbors in their patios, frightened to death and trying to imagine a world without General Manuel Noriega. Meanwhile, on a nearby US military base, US officials were secretly installing Guillermo Endara[1] in office as Panama's first post-invasion civilian president. The United States did whisk Noriega far away to a US jail, but left Endara to face an economy in shambles, with a huge foreign debt. To help steer the way, Endara appointed a cabinet that included members of the country's white oligarchy who had been purged from political control during Panama's two decades of military rule. Wealthy civilian elites were back in power.

Panama's civilian governments of the 1990s, like their military predecessors, turned to the US and international lenders for even more loans. As before, their compliance with lenders' "neoliberal demands" was often at the expense of the majority of Panamanians. Working people, for example, were hurt by new labor policies and reforms making it easier for employers to move workers around, reduce their hours, or fire them. Indigenous peoples' rights were threatened by government concessions to foreign companies of mining rights on Indigenous lands. A World Bank report in 1999[2] described Panama as a country where "the poorest are very poor and the richest very rich," where income inequality was among the highest in the world. Living in poverty were 37 percent of Panamanians, including half the country's children. Panamanians protested their government's neoliberal policies during the 1990s through mass demonstrations, boycotts, and strikes.

like Loma Bonita and wanted David to bring her here, although he'd warned her about the steep slopes to climb by foot and lack of electricity or indoor plumbing. When she came, I put on a nice dress, even shoes, but what Mariela noticed was my bleeding nose sore. She proposed to take me for an examination by a doctor she knew in Penonomé. "And, the money?" I'd asked her. "Don't worry," she'd said, "I can arrange it." David insisted, too, and I couldn't say no to my son.

That's how Esperanza did finally "get cut," first for a biopsy by Penonomé doctors and then by cancer specialists in Panama City. Mariela made the initial arrangements, and Esperanza's son Tony was able to insure his mother's health through his construction job. As a low-income senior, Esperanza paid only a $20 fee for five days in the hospital.

Now, three months after the operation, she's still under the care of her daughters in El Mirador while Andrés guards their home in Loma Bonita. Esperanza's face is still animated by her dark eyes and ever-active protruding lower lip, but the inch-long, red scar beside her nose distorts it a little. A small price to pay.

~

The big day has arrived. David's ordination. Before daybreak in El Mirador, 20 of us pile into the family's privately rented green and white bus headed to the church in Penonomé; Andrés will meet us there. Anticipation fills the air. Esperanza is wearing a new emerald green cotton dress designed and sewn by Lety. She wanted to wear green, she tells me, "because it means hope, the hope I've carried all this time for David's success."

By 8:30, we're at the church where more than 500 people are crammed into a small, outside area; many are from Loma Bonita. I count one archbishop and bishop and about 30 priests decked out in crisp white robes. Sweat runs like water as we wait and wait for the president of Panama to arrive. Then the pomp and circumstance begin. I whisper to Esperanza and Andrés, "David looks very handsome with his dark hair, mustache, and full beard. He's the first university graduate to have been born and raised in Loma Bonita." They beam.

~

A week later, we sit in the stifling hot air outside Loma Bonita's small church where hundreds of people are jammed into a tiny space. Among them, young highland migrants who've come from the city decked out in trendy urban fashions featuring lots of bare skin and tennis shoes, a far cry from the apparel of even a decade ago. For the past month,

**BOX 5.2 A WIDER LENS: 1999 – THE UNITED STATES RETURNS THE PANAMA CANAL**

At noon on December 31, 1999, as stipulated in the Torrijos-Carter treaty of 1977, the United States returned the Panama Canal to Panama as well as $30 billion of associated property, and all US military installations. On that day, Mireya Moscoso, Panama's recently elected president, shouted "The Canal is Ours," as she hoisted the Panamanian flag up over the administration building in the formerly US-controlled Canal Zone. Actually, Panamanians had been successfully administering the Canal for a decade; more than 70 percent of canal managers and most floating equipment operators were already Panamanians.[3] Many hoped that this marked the end of more than a century of US imperialism in their country.

Far away in Loma Bonita, Father David listens to the ceremony on his radio. He's feeling joyful and proud of Panama. No one else in the family pays much attention to the event; they're busy working.

many people from near and far have dug, sawed, cut, hammered, nailed, planted, and harvested to prepare for this day when Father David will give his first mass. Several have told me how excited they are that a man who grew up in these mountains and understands what life is really like has reached such an esteemed position as "Father." Said one, "This feels like we're making history." One bishop, a monsignor, and about 20 priests are already here when the pickup truck finally delivers David and another priest. Soon David stands before us on the pulpit, white robe against coal black beard. Except for babies' cries, it gets quiet. He gives the mass. I'm surprised by how deep, sometimes booming, his voice has become. Father David is coming into his own.

## 2001 – MOTHER NATALIA'S LONG JOURNEY

I've just returned to Loma Bonita from Panama City on this sunny February day, and I get the bad news from Tina. Without hesitation, I run to Andrés and Esperanza's house where Esperanza greets me in the patio wearing a grim face. Pointing her protruding lower lip toward the house, she says, "Mama's inside in the small bedroom." I go inside and pull back the curtain that serves as a door to a very small, urine-scented room with only a bed and a few stacks of cartons along a wall. In the dim light, I see that 98-year-old Natalia Ruiz is sitting up in the bed. She sees me and smiles. "Oh, it's you," she says. "How are you?"

I'm happy and surprised that she remembers me. She's had major memory problems for the past few years and didn't recall my name when I last saw her. But then she asks, "Where did you leave your horse?" Clearly she has no idea who I am. I move closer so she can hear me. Her hearing has been failing for two decades, and by now conversations come in shouts.

"How are you?" I yell. She's staring at my black leather belt, which is at the level of her eyes.

"What's that?" she shouts back.

"A belt."

"Do you have any money?" she asks.

"No."

I sit on the edge of the bed and take her hand. "Sra. Natalia, I'm so sorry that you had a bad fall."

"Thank you, dear, I'll rest now," she says, and closes her eyes.

I join Esperanza and Andrés outside near the kitchen and describe the conversation. Despite the grave situation, we fall into irrepressible laughter over "the possible location of my horse." We reminisce about Natalia's vigorous life. I recall how impressed I was in 1993 watching 90-year-old Natalia climbing the steep slopes between Frailecito and Loma Bonita. But later in the 1990s, Esperanza remembers,

> Mama lost her ability to walk and climb. So we sisters and brothers got together and decided she couldn't live alone; we'd take turns caring for her for five months each.

Then one day during Esperanza's brother's turn to take care of Natalia, she "escaped" from his house. A neighbor found her hours later wandering around the stream, scantily dressed. Esperanza went home and told Andrés. His advice: "Bring her here. What we eat, she will too."

But Natalia's presence in their house greatly complicated their lives. For the past decade, Esperanza and Andrés had been taking turns going to El Mirador to help Viviana and Lety, both single parents. After all, Esperanza had said, someone had to guard their houses from thieves when they went to work. And someone had to take care of the two new babies that arrived in 1998 and 1999, when Lety, as well as Viviana's daughter Isabel, both gave birth to sons. Now, with Natalia in their care, Esperanza and Andrés sometimes had to bring her along to the city.

When I visited the family in El Mirador in late 1999, Natalia was there. Esperanza's turn in the city was coming to an end, and Andrés would soon replace her. Esperanza was ready to go home to Loma Bonita, "I'm tired of the constant noise of tied-up dogs barking conversations to each other," she told me.

"But when you're in Loma Bonita now, you'll be all alone," I pointed out.

"Yes, but tranquil, content to watch my squawking hens and chicks," she said, standing up to imitate them by flapping and squawking for a moment. But then she became serious:

> If I die alone some night, God will be there. I've already planned for my funeral. Andrés's nephew Narciso will build the coffin and dig the hole. Tina and my other neighbor, Nella, will kill and cook chickens and notify my children about costs. They know to bury me quickly and not wait for my children who might not have enough money to get there fast.

~

Weeks later, when Andrés was on duty in El Mirador, Natalia asked nonstop to be taken back to her house and *monte* in Loma Bonita. He finally conceded and brought her "home." But things didn't go well. "She's gotten out of control," Esperanza had told me one February day in 2000.

> Last night Andrés caught her lighting matches, and, when I scolded her, she tried to hit me. She said, "I want to go back to my own house where no one scolds me, where I can make great big *bollos nuevo* [buns made from new corn] whenever I want." Andrés says he can't take care of her anymore. When I go to the city, I'll have to take her with me.

I ask, "Wouldn't it be easier to just stay here in Loma Bonita with her?" She responds, "But then who will help out my daughters so they can work?"

Esperanza left her mother with Viviana and Lety in El Mirador in Panama City during the next year, and stayed there herself much of the time. But Natalia never ceased to beseech everyone to take her back to Loma Bonita, and Esperanza decided in February of 2001 to heed her mother's pleas. The return trip was tricky. They had to carry Natalia down a very steep dirt path from the house in El Mirador to the top of an ultra-steep, rickety stone stairway (see Figure 5.2). Then they had to get her down many stairs to my car, waiting at the top of an ultra-steep paved road. In this, we succeeded and got to Copé, the end of the road for my small car. And, although the wait in Copé for a passenger car to Loma Bonita was long and the afternoon air like the inside of a brutally hot sauna, Natalia arrived in Loma Bonita that day.

It was soon after this return to Loma Bonita that Natalia got out of bed in the middle of the night and had the terrible fall that brought me running to their house today to visit her. She's still in too much pain to get out of bed.

Esperanza and Andrés, almost 80, can't attend to many of Natalia's needs, so, as soon as she can be moved, Lety has offered to take care of her grandmother in El Mirador for two months. Lety is currently unemployed but earning money as a seamstress from home while taking care of her baby son and nephew. I'm hoping that, with Lety's loving care, the next time I visit Natalia she'll be content to be in El Mirador, and remember that I don't have a horse.

It takes Esperanza a few minutes to remember where she is when she first opens her eyes on this August morning in El Mirador. This is because she now travels every two weeks between Loma Bonita and El Mirador where her mother is in the full-time care of Lety and Viviana. For a week now, Esperanza has been in the city, pleased that Natalia seems stable although in need of help to do everything. Not long ago, I asked Esperanza about the things in her life for which she was most thankful. High up on her list was, "My mother is still with me, a bit crazy, but here."

**Figure 5.2. Helping Natalia down steep stairs to go from El Mirador to Loma Bonita, 2001.**

Esperanza dresses and walks the 10 feet from Lety's, where she sleeps, to Viviana's house where Natalia is still in bed. With help from Sebastián, Viviana's oldest son, Esperanza bathes Natalia and dresses her in a blue housedress. Her mother eats a good breakfast of bread, coffee, and an egg.

The sun is strong when Lety, Esperanza, and Sebastián help Natalia move to an area in the patio between the two houses where the family has arranged a table, several chairs, a sewing machine, and a small bed for Natalia's daytime naps. This way, Lety can do her sewing without leaving Natalia alone.

At dinner, Natalia has a hard time swallowing her rice, so Sebastián comes to the rescue with some yogurt that she likes. Soon it's bedtime, and Sebastián takes his great-grandmother to the room she shares with him and his mother. Viviana is now back from work. "Grandmother," she says, "let's go to sleep." Natalia smiles. It's 10 p.m.

Viviana has strong dreams about her grandmother. At 3 a.m. she wakes up, as she does every night, to help Natalia urinate. "Grandmother, get up," she whispers, touching her lightly. No response. She tries again. No response. Then, it hits her. Her grandmother isn't breathing. She died in her sleep. Viviana goes running with her sorrow to Lety's house.

Tears, chaos, and haste follow, while everyone tries to figure out what to do. As there is no telephone nearby, the first priority is to contact the rest of the family. Lety and her husband run to the nearby police station to report the death, and they use its telephone to call Lety's Aunt María and brother David who, in turn, will get the word to Tony and to Andrés in Loma Bonita.

On this Saturday morning in El Mirador – August 25 – the whole family is in motion. Lety would later tell me, "We were all in such despair. God did his bidding, and we hadn't even had a cup of coffee to help us run around with our grief."

Viviana's older daughter, Isabel, gets on a bus to Colón to bring her Aunt Sophia back to El Mirador. Lety runs to her nearby church to cancel her commitments, and then catches a bus to her Aunt María's apartment to commiserate and plan for the funeral. Once home again, Lety remembers about "the dress." Many years before, her grandmother had told her this: "When I die, I'd like to be buried in a white dress that covers my feet and has long sleeves." Lety rushes out again to buy the material to sew this dress. When later she and Viviana comb Natalia's hair and put on her long white dress, it fits beautifully. Just like she wanted.

Meanwhile, getting Natalia to the morgue is a priority. David had instructed them to contact the police to get her there. When the police come, they wrap Natalia's body in a sheet and carry her down the steep hill and stairway to their truck. Family members follow behind and witness the saddest moment of all. As Tony later told me, "Those two policemen just slung grandmother's body up onto the back of their truck as though she was a sack of yuca, a dog. We all cried when they left."

Sophia and several others have a different task. They've recruited a relative with a car to get them to a funeral home. They buy the cheapest coffin for $150, but can't afford a hearse to take Natalia's body to Loma

Bonita for burial. Instead, David finds an acquaintance with a pickup truck; for $100, he'll take Natalia home to Loma Bonita on Monday. In the midst of all these necessary tasks, a steady stream of relatives and friends from the city congregate in El Mirador on Saturday and Sunday. Esperanza, her children, and their children are cooking, serving, crying, laughing, and telling stories.

On Monday, Viviana, Lety, and Tony climb into the pickup truck that carries their grandmother's casket in the back. When they get to Esperanza and Andrés's house in Loma Bonita, the aroma of coffee and murmur of people float through the air. Andrés is cooking soup.

All night long, the family is cooking *bollos* and other foods, preparing for tomorrow's prayer session and then burial down in the cemetery. People come to view the body, recite prayers, and say goodbye to Natalia Ruiz Herrera. Born on July 3, 1901, before Panama was even a country, she lived to be 100, the oldest person in Loma Bonita, and maybe in the whole region. She left behind 6 living children, 30 grandchildren, and all of their children. Sophia would later tell me "I was grateful that God gave my grandmother 100 years and that she died in peace."

I, too, was thankful for the flood of memories Natalia left behind – like the times I'd go to her house and stay the night. She taught me how to roll and smoke black tobacco, and we'd talk the night away. Natalia gifted me a "saying" from her generation that has instructed me ever since: "Little by little the old woman eats the coconut, even though she has no teeth."

Months later, Esperanza calculated the costs of Natalia's funeral to have been about $500, plus hundreds more in food. Donations from many relatives and friends provided almost $300 as well as much food. "Luckily," she told me, "Andrés and I had almost $400 in savings, most in the bank account that David helped us open last year. If not, we would have had to bury Mama in the city, and she couldn't have come home to rest in peace."

## 2011 – ESPERANZA AND HUSBAND ANDRÉS AT 90

As I approach Esperanza and Andrés's house for breakfast on this bright February morning with cloudless pale blue sky, I'm remembering what

Esperanza once said about her house: "In this old adobe house where I live, people will come to my wake." She was wrong. Instead of that three-room adobe house, she and Andrés now live in a cement-block home with a sitting room and four bedrooms. At the back of the house is a small, indoor kitchen with an earth floor. Outside, next to the kitchen, is a tiny rigged-up shower, closeted by three walls of metal roofing sheets and a white plastic curtain for "privacy." The old outdoor kitchen still stands with its waist-high woodstove, as does the outhouse, accessed by the same steep, difficult descent on rough, uneven stones. Their daughter Sophia's husband, José – a construction worker – built this house in 2007, with help from various family members. It was paid for with contributions from Esperanza and Andrés's children and with money from the sale of Andrés's small coffee farm. Electricity has still not arrived in Loma Bonita, and cell-phone signals reach only the highest hills, but in this house, thanks again to contributions from children, are two light outlets and a TV, powered by a solar panel that José installed.

*"Oiy, Oiy,"* I yell out when I arrive. As always, Esperanza and Andrés return my call from inside the house. Andrés comes out to greet me. Work-hunched and still skinny as a rail at almost 90 years old, he's wearing gray baggy pants, an old orange shirt turned inside out, sandals, and a frayed straw hat that covers some still-black hair.

"How do you feel this morning," I ask, noticing how his eyes have turned blue-gray with age.

"*Ave Maria*, my left knee hurts. And this other one, too. And my feet, like they're on fire. I woke up twice last night and put on a menthol rub so I could go back to sleep."

He tells me about his dream.

> Death came to my bed and lay down. She wore white. I touched her, and she was all bones. But she didn't touch me. A friend told me this wasn't death; he said death is grey and touches you. In my dream, heaven was beautiful, a huge mansion where you get to see everyone who's gone.

Andrés is weaker each time I come; a 10-minute walk to the community store now leaves him short of breath. He's not been able to work regularly in his *monte* or orange grove for almost 20 years, but has never stopped yearning to be there. Despite falls, which worry his children, he still tries to tend to light farm tasks near the house, and he walks around with his machete tied around his waist. In addition to a 10-year-old bad cough that his healer hasn't cured, he's battling diminishing eyesight and hearing. But his sense of humor is intact. After describing the beauty of heaven, he smiles playfully, "But I'd rather be here in this ugly world."

Esperanza calls us to the kitchen for breakfast. She has more energy than during my last field trip when she had a urinary tract infection and cough. She says she feels good, despite a fall while harvesting yuca a few months ago that broke a rib. Recently, she proved her prowess. Her son Tony and cousin María had been visiting from the capital and were preparing to go back there with oranges from Esperanza's orchard. Tony had just left to take his sacks to the road, to await a car to Copé. María, aged 81, tried to lift her 25-pound sack, but couldn't. Nor could I help because my hands were still bandaged from a recent surgery. So Esperanza grabbed the whole sack, hoisted it up on her shoulder, and remarkably got it to the road. She's 89.

Andrés and I sit on wooden benches outside the kitchen, and Esperanza serves us boiled yuca and a fried egg. "Good morning," yells Nella from the front door. "Come on in," we yell back to this neighbor, who was recently hired by Esperanza and Andrés's children to help the couple for a few hours each morning and afternoon. For $80 a month, Nella is expected to do some cooking and cleaning and to provide a watchful eye and company; she's a lively 50-year-old who loves to talk and jokes easily. And she's strong; last week I saw her descending a steep slope with a 50-pound sack of oranges on her back.

Caring for Esperanza and Andrés has become a major challenge for their five children. None can come live in Loma Bonita permanently. All still work, except Viviana who retired due to ill health, but she takes care of grandchildren in the city. Neither do Esperanza or Andrés want to move to the city; they like to visit, but then they want to return to their chickens and house, "to our land, our home." To complicate this further, Esperanza and Andrés are not getting along. Old grudges have led to fighting between them, leaving their children trying to figure out how to either separate them or keep them together but accompanied by someone else. They hope Nella's presence can suffice.

## 2011 – WHEN LAND BECOMES CAPITALIST PROPERTY AS WELL AS "HOME"

During this field trip in 2011, I'm focused on learning about the sale of Loma Bonita's land to lowlanders. These sales began about a decade ago when the government widened, smoothed, and then put asphalt on the road leading west from Copé up to Loma Bonita and beyond. Despite a myriad of construction problems that followed, this two-lane paved road opened the door for major changes in these mountains, including in the control of land. Lowlanders with money to spare began eyeing this highland area as a place for themselves. It was cooler up here, with stunning vistas, especially on the highest part of the slopes, called the ***cerro***. And there were plenty of very poor people who'd be willing to sell them cheap land – perfect for an investment or second home as a "residential tourist."

Potential lowland buyers started showing up, a situation I witnessed while visiting Cristino Blanco two years ago in 2009.[4] We were in the patio of his three-room cement-block house that sat near the entrance to one of Loma Bonita's *cerros*. Suddenly we heard the unlikely sound of a car engine slowly descending the steep dirt path that wound down from higher up in that *cerro* and passed his house. A black, four-wheel-drive SUV, as wide as the path itself, stopped where we were sitting. The blackened window creaked down, and a man wearing shades yelled out, "Do you have any land for sale? No one was home at the house above you." Cristino yelled back: "Not today. Maybe later." The blackened window went up, and the man drove away.

At that time in 2009, Cristino was one of 11 community members – 8 men and 3 women – who had sold parcels of their land to 26 different lowlanders, most of whom were wealthy merchants or professional Panamanians from the capital or a Coclé lowland town. Cristino had already made five or six of these land sales, ranging from a few hundred square meters (12 square meters are about the size of a car parking space) to eight hectares (almost 20 acres). His reasons for selling were similar to those of the other 10. As he put it,

> I know that some people are against selling. They say it's wrong to let strangers – who could even be drug traffickers – take over our land. But tell me, Gloria, what's a 77-year-old man supposed

> to do? I can't work anymore, but we have needs. With money from these sales, I built this house, got pipes for running water inside and out, and paid for my hernia operation. And at my age, what did I have to lose by selling land way up there in the *cerro* where I couldn't plant anyway? My children and grandchildren live in Panama City, and won't be coming back to stay.

"Who, then, will live in Loma Bonita in ten years?" I asked Cristino. He shrugged his shoulders.

Two years later, in 2011, I've come to Loma Bonita to explore the impacts of these land sales on community life. When I arrive at Esperanza and Andrés's for breakfast today, Esperanza is already dressed and ready to leave. She and Tina had asked to accompany me on my visit to one of several *cerro* areas in Loma Bonita where lowlanders are continuing to buy land and build houses. Esperanza wears a bright royal blue dress and lime-green crocs with a hole on top that she cut out for air. "You look pretty," I say. "No bra," she brags. "I no longer worry about such things." We eat quickly, and leave to pick up Tina.

I'm tickled to have their company on this sightseeing foray, and love, too, to witness their growing friendship. Since Francisco died of a massive asthma attack in 2001, Tina and Esperanza have become closer. They visit and help one another out and do things together. Just last week, they joined others on a bus to Penonomé to protest the imminent firing of a Loma Bonita teacher. The next day they traveled together by car to a nearby community to join a protest against a government decision about the municipal office.

We three walk to the paved road and luckily get a car ride quickly to the entrance to this *cerro* area. From there, we climb a steep dirt path with an asphalt strip in the middle, built by lowlanders so they can drive to their new properties without passing the houses of Loma Bonita residents.

The view is gorgeous way up here among the tall pine trees. We walk and talk freely, since lowlanders aren't here on weekdays. Tina, being Tina, starts to giggle and sing right away. She belts out a song she created in my honor a decade ago; it describes her *pena* (embarrassment) when I first arrived and how our relationship over time has helped her overcome it. I've been told she sings this every time new students or US Peace Corps workers come to Loma Bonita.[5]

**BOX 5.3 A WIDER LENS: TOURISM IN CENTRAL AMERICA AND PANAMA SINCE 2000**

In 2012, the *New York Times* travel section highlighted Panama as a desirable tourist destination by awarding it first place on its list of "the 45 Places to Go"; again in 2019, Panama won fourth place on the news agency's list of "52 Places to Go."[6] Tourism has been a key source of national revenue, gross national product (GNP), and foreign exchange in most Latin American countries since the 1990s,[7] and in Central America, since about 2000. Panama has been at the forefront of this more recent explosive growth.[8] International moneylenders, like the World Bank and the IMF, have been behind the push to promote tourism everywhere, demanding that, in exchange for their loans, countries get rid of barriers to foreign trade and welcome global service industries, such as tourism.

Panama's governments have complied, introducing beach tourism, heritage tourism, ecotourism, and especially, as elsewhere in Central America, "residential tourism." In an effort to attract retirees, especially wealthy foreigners, to come make a home on the isthmus as residential tourists – as well as developers to build these homes – the government created incentives, such as easy visa requirements, health care discounts, tax breaks, and permission to export profits out of Panama.[9]

These measures have paid off. In 2009, tourism, including residential tourism, was generating as much income as the Panama Canal; by 2014, almost twice as much.[10] But who have been the beneficiaries? From studies done in two areas that the Panamanian government has targeted for residential tourism – the mountains of Boquete and beaches of Bocas del Toro – enormous wealth has gone mostly to foreigners and elite Panamanians. Many poor local residents have instead faced skyrocketing land and housing prices, a higher cost of living, traffic jams, and deteriorated water and sewage systems, as well as growing class inequality and conflicts in their daily lives.[11] Is this to be Loma Bonita's future, too?

As we climb, conversation moves easily from trees and plants to money and politics. Tina says, "Aunt Esperanza, I bought a good mattress with my '70s money' last week." She's referring to the $100 that the current government of President Martinelli gives monthly to everyone over 70 years old who qualifies as being "poor and without a pension."[12] "Us, too," says Esperanza:

> With our very first payment last year we bought a new mattress for David. Then we went to the super[market] and pharmacy for Andrés's medicines, and later paid workers to harvest our oranges. It was like a party. I thank Martinelli every day for helping us out. No one ever did before.

This thought leads Esperanza down memory lane.

> Remember the Torrijos days when Uncle Cristo was running for representative and we formed committee after committee? What happened? Nothing changed. Next came that church food coop that took our time and money, until it went down just like the Torrijos one. Then came Mireya [Moscoso] in '99; we all worked so hard to get her elected president. When she won, I said to Andrés, "If she doesn't help us, I'll never believe in anyone again. Maybe I'll never vote." Well, Mireya did nothing for us either.
>
> But, finally, now we have Martinelli.

Tina agrees, but raises the problem of rising food and gas prices under Martinelli. And, she says, she saw on TV when she was visiting her children in the city that he's doing "bad things to poor Indians."

We reach the end of the path high up on this *cerro* and have counted seven lots owned by lowlanders, each with a fence around the property. (Figure 5.3 compares the house of Esperanza and Andrés with that of one resident tourist from the lowlands.) On four lots, owners have built one- or two-story houses, positioned to catch magnificent views from windows. A woman from Loma Bonita is sweeping the pavement at one house, and she lets us peek inside. We marvel at the tiled floors, modern bathroom, and kitchen appliances powered by a private generator.

**Figure 5.3. The house of Esperanza and Andrés (above) and the house of one resident tourist (below), 2007.**

"It's hard to believe we're in Loma Bonita," says Tina.

"We'll never sell land to these people," Esperanza responds. "Where would our children go?"

~

At dinner tonight, Andrés's much-loved nephew Narciso shows up. This now 65-year-old man lives nearby and has always helped them with agricultural and household work. This assistance has become even more important as Andrés and Esperanza have aged, not only because their children are far away but also due to the increasing difficulty of finding laborers for *juntas* or even for paid day work. Almost all young women are away working, and most young men now also migrate to urban or other rural areas to earn salaries; those who stay in the community, like Narciso, move between their own fields and Coclé's lowland plantations during much of the year. Luckily, he's always given some priority to the needs of Andrés and Esperanza, often showing up at the end of the day to check on things. Like today.

Because Narciso is such a trusted family member, I feel free to bring up the sensitive subject of land. I say,

> Esperanza, this morning you said you'd never sell land to lowlanders, but I remember that a few years ago you told me you were thinking about selling them a plot of your *cerro* land because you considered it useless for agriculture.

Andrés responds, "But our children said 'no.' Viviana told us, 'Don't even think it.' They all said they didn't know about the future, but maybe they'd want to come back here to live." Esperanza adds, "I'm glad now we didn't do it." She goes on to explain why she changed her mind.

> These land sales are pulling families apart. Look what happened to my poor cousin Felipa. First, she sold some lowlander land near her house in the *cerro*, excited to have a good neighbor close by. But instead, he built a fence that blocked Felipa from getting to her water tank. Then, her children started fighting among themselves. Some said don't sell; others went ahead and sold lots to lowlanders. Everyone's angry. There've been fistfights

> and lawsuits. All over land and money. Poor Felipa is alone up there now, with almost no land left.

Narciso joins in:

> Let's face it; we sell to lowlanders even though they pay almost nothing for our land. It just seems like a lot to us because we have so little money and so much need. They get away with it because we don't have legal land titles.

To back up his point, he rattles off a few examples. Raúl Ortiz sold his lot for $4,000 to a lowlander who resold it immediately to another outsider for more than $20,000. And Pancho Ruiz sold a lot to a lowlander for $500 who then built a big house and got over $60,000 for it.

"But we're learning," Narciso goes on.

> People in Loma Bonita are asking for more money, even if it's still much less than the real value. In the beginning some sold a square meter (.0002 acres) for $1.50; now it's hard to find anyone selling for less than $6.

Esperanza takes issue: "But this just raises the cost of land for us all." She recalls that her stepbrother bought land for $20 a hectare (2.5 acres) in the 1950s, and even in the 1970s, she and Andrés paid his two uncles only $160 for about three hectares.

> But now most of us can't afford to buy. A few years ago, Tina was shocked to learn that a neighbor was asking $10,000 for a plot of less than one hectare. She wanted it, but couldn't afford it.

After several more stories about how hikes in land prices have hurt local people, Andrés mentions that a similar thing is happening with laborers. Some lowlanders are now paying $10 a day here instead of the usual $7, he says, "making it even harder for people like us to get day workers." Narciso grins sheepishly, and I know why. Earlier this month, he and his brother agreed to work for a few weeks for a lowlander instead of for Andrés who was paying $3 less. They did promise to come work for Andrés later, but it might be too late to prepare his field for planting. Andrés continues his complaint:

> So now we have to pay workers more or go without enough help in our fields. There's no community spirit [*convivencia*] anymore. No one does anything without payment, and there are hardly any *juntas*. Often you can't get workers to help, not even for money.

I've never heard Andrés sound so cynical.

## 2017 – HUSBAND ANDRÉS'S TREASURED LIFE

I'm feeling happy on this ninth day of January, sitting in the chilly Atlanta airport. My life in Pittsburgh is behind me for a few months, the warmth of Panama ahead. *Ding* goes my cell phone. There's a WhatsApp message from David who knows I'll be in Loma Bonita soon. It says, "Papa died this morning."

No, no! Andrés couldn't leave without saying goodbye, without giving the two of us time to sit side by side in the patio at sunset, as we did two years ago, enjoying the quiet, the orange and mango trees, and the yellow hibiscus, conversation no longer necessary. He was already leaving us then, sleeping much of the day. Sometimes he knew me, sometimes not. But if I moved really close to him and said hello, he'd smile broadly and say, "Gloria, when did you get here? Will you stay awhile?"

I remember him in his 50s and 60s, always moving, graceful, a radiant smile and calm voice making me feel protected and safe. One evening in 1984 during a fierce rainy season, my 10-year-old son Reid and I left his house after dinner to go to Tina and Francisco's for the night. We ploughed through soggy coffee trees and mud, but got stuck at the stream. The water was high and running so swiftly that I was terrified to try to cross while holding my son. Back I went to get Andrés who waded into the stream arms outstretched and carried Reid to the other side. There were few people in this world to whom I would have surrendered my precious son in the midst of that raging stream.

~

At the mass for Andrés this morning, about 200 people and 12 priests are packed into Loma Bonita's small church; at the pulpit, tears abundant, is Father David. Afterwards, Esperanza's house is packed: people are everywhere, even in the new indoor bathroom, a $3,000 gift from a rich lowland woman, a devout Catholic who wanted to help Father David's elderly parents. There are so many people in Esperanza's patio that I don't see her when I arrive. But there she is, surrounded by her 5 children, 15 grandchildren, their children, and others from the city as well as relatives and neighbors from Loma Bonita. She's sitting there, looking distant. I go over and hug her. She says, "Andrés said you were more like a daughter." In the kitchen, the sitting room, the bedrooms, and the patio people are telling stories about Andrés, shedding tears and laughing over the funny things he'd say. When I leave with Tina for the night, I count 30 people who will sleep at Esperanza's house – in beds or hammocks, on chairs or floors in the patio. I recall what Andrés told me 15 years ago, when I asked if he considered himself to be "poor."

> Yes, poor in health. I used to like to carry wood and cook in fiestas, but now with this cough and my failing body, I can't. But in esteem, I'm not poor. I have equal affection for everyone. When I go out, I have many friends.

The crowded gatherings in his church and home give testimony to Andrés Blanco Soto as a family and community treasure. He was 94.

## 2017 – ESPERANZA BATTLES BACK FROM LOSS

A month later, I climb those last rocks onto Esperanza's patio, ready for breakfast. She's sitting at the table outside but doesn't run over to greet me as always. I'm worried about Esperanza. Since the funeral, she spends her days sitting, eating, sleeping, and watching TV, now that electricity has made its way into her home, like most others. I don't recognize this lethargic woman.

Viviana is nearby watering the flowers. I can hear Sophia in the kitchen, and the clack, clack of spoon against cup. For the past two years, these two daughters have been alternating – spending three-month stints in Loma Bonita to care for their parents. Before then, Andrés and Esperanza's four urban children had moved them from one to another of their homes. But when Andrés fell out of bed and was hospitalized in 2015, they agreed that their parents had to stay in one place and get constant attention. That one place is Loma Bonita, "home," where both wanted to be.

But who could come live with them for months at a time? That was the question. Not Tony, the construction worker, still helping to support his five grown children and their spouses and babies in Panama City. Nor could David, the priest, leave his work to live in Loma Bonita, although his church was within an hour of the community, and he came regularly to check on his parents. Lety, like her brothers, couldn't leave her business for long. A decade ago, she and her husband had moved from the capital to a small city in central Panama to live near his sister and open an outdoor food stall. Their tiny business, which they named The Sun Comes Out For Everyone (El Sol Sale Para Todos), did well, and by 2015 had become three adjacent stalls offering fruits, vegetables, cooked foods, and all manner of inexpensive household goods and plastic trinkets. Their continued success depended on their sunup to sundown labor. Besides, Lety had a school-aged son and granddaughter to care for.

The commitment to come to Loma Bonita to take care of Andrés and Esperanza, therefore, fell to Viviana and Sophia. Not that they could easily leave their urban homes. Both now lived near one another in a rural area not far from Colón City. Although Viviana no longer had a man in her life, she was still helping to raise two grandchildren. And Sophia's house was full of people who needed her, including her husband José and four grown children with spouses and babies. José was not always happy with her long absences. Sophia explained,

> At first, he'd say, "You aren't their only child. Why do you have to be the one to go?" "Look at me," I told him. "Who I am, what I am, is thanks to them. If you want to find another woman, well, go ahead." He said, "You're right, you need to go." But at Christmas, again he said, "Not another Christmas away from here." I told him I didn't know if my parents would even be here next Christmas. He understood and decided to come to Loma Bonita for Christmas with gifts for the kids. He liked it here with all the visits you get daily from family and neighbors.

After breakfast, I bid farewell for the day to Sophia and Viviana. But where is Esperanza? Viviana tells me her mother has gone back to bed. What? It's only 10 a.m. Viviana and I have a talk about Esperanza's depressed state and agree on a strategy to get her moving: I'll invite her to come with me today as I go from house to house visiting people. I go to Esperanza's bedroom and ask if she's interested. Yes. No hesitation. Fifteen minutes later, Esperanza emerges ready to go, dressed up in a mint green jacket, tan dress, store-bought straw hat, and white crocs.

Esperanza suggests we take a path through orange groves rather than the main road, and I soon learn her motive. "This is Lety's new orange grove that she bought from our neighbor, Daniel. I've wanted to check it out." As we walk, Esperanza notices everything.

> Look at that tree still loaded with oranges that they haven't harvested. And look at these damaged tree trunks; it's the plague. Lety will have to fumigate here.

We keep walking. "Oh, look over there. That banana plant has fallen to the ground from the winds. There must be 30 bananas that need to be harvested quickly."

We come to the end of Lety's property, marked by a fence with three barbed wires. It seems too high to climb over and too low to climb under. I say, "Looks like we'll have to go back."

"No Gloria, we can get under here. Just hold this bottom wire up as high as you can."

To my surprise and delight, Esperanza gets down on the ground and slides her chubby body under that wire. It was very close. She scuttles up and holds the wire for me. I can't believe she really just did this, 94-year-old Esperanza.

After visits with three families, we head home. Esperanza guides us through a different part of Lety's new orange grove where there isn't even a path. Along the way she describes the condition of this and that tree, bush, plant, flower, bird. We get to a mandarin tree, and she stops, looks up, and sees a few mandarins that she thinks are good.

"I'm going to get them," she says, and before I can protest, she climbs onto a big rock; takes off her shoes; reaches up, up to catch a limb; and shakes it to free the fruit. Two mandarins crash down, and we peel with enthusiasm. They're totally dry. We fall into uncontrolled laughter.

Viviana is waiting for us back at the house. She's a little worried, as we've been gone for four hours. Esperanza looks excited, like she's just been on a great adventure. Her eyes are aglow, and she's telling stories energetically. For today, at least, Esperanza is back.

## 2017 – NEIGHBORS OR ENEMIES? LOWLANDERS IN LOMA BONITA

I always enjoy hanging out with others here in front of Victoriano Ortiz's small store by the paved road. Today it's quieter than usual because it's Sunday and fewer cars and trucks with squeaky brakes and loud horns pass by on their way up and down the mountain. Suddenly, the small roar of a bright green motorbike interrupts the quiet. My ride has arrived. Antonio Ortiz, Victoriano's cousin (and an ex–Delegate of the Word), offered to give me a tour of the homes of lowlanders who have bought land on the *cerro* where he lives, the same area that Esperanza, Tina, and I had explored in 2011.

The motorbike gets us there in no time. We pass a quaint-looking house with a round outdoor patio. "This used to be my land," says Antonio, "until about 15 years ago when a lowland acquaintance asked me as a favor to sell this lot to a friend who needed a quiet place to build a cabin." Antonio complied, and at a very cheap price. "But what a mistake," he says. Not only did the new owner not build a cabin, but he resold the land at considerable profit to a lowland woman who built this house, which she almost never visits. Antonio assumes she'll eventually resell it for a big return and worries about who will be his next neighbor. He swears that neither he nor his siblings will sell to lowlanders again.

The sale of Loma Bonita's land to lowlanders continues, but at an unhurried pace because the region has not (yet) been targeted by the government for "residential tourism." Information about land for sale still moves mainly by word of mouth. Also, some community members won't sell now either because they've gotten burned, like Antonio, or are saving land for children, as Esperanza is doing. Others who do sell, like one of Antonio's cousins, distinguish between people like himself, who sell out of necessity, and those who "just want to get rich."

By the time Antonio and I reach the top of this slope, we've passed nine lots of land now owned by lowlanders, six with houses already built or under construction. This makes two more lots and houses than in 2011 on this one *cerro*. At one house, we see a man getting out of his truck. "Good afternoon, Salvador," Antonio hollers, and the man beckons us to come up to the patio of his two-story cement-block and stone house. As we approach, Antonio whispers that Salvador works in a lowland town for an important politician. We are treated very amiably and offered a Coca-Cola and crackers. Salvador tells us that he hopes to retire here someday.

Antonio has to leave for a short time, and in his absence, Salvador shifts the conversation and the tone. He tells me about how hard he worked in his town to bring water and electricity to Loma Bonita and "these people." Without him, he seems to be saying, it would not have happened. While I believe he made an effort to get these modern amenities to the community where he now has a house, I'm remembering the 25-year struggle undertaken by so many community members to reach this goal. Antonio returns, and Salvador changes the subject to the benefits his family has brought to Coclé Province. When we leave, I tell Antonio that Salvador took credit for Loma Bonita's water and electricity advances. "Oh," he responds, "Salvador does like to brag."

Almost two decades after lowlanders began buying lots in Loma Bonita, I see no evidence of interest on their part to get to know the community or its residents. Antonio agrees, "When they arrive in Loma Bonita, most go right to their private entrances and stay on their property until they leave" – except for one woman whom Antonio praises for being "a nice person who brought gifts for community children last Christmas."

In general, Loma Bonita residents and lowland property owners interact not as neighbors and social equals but as poor farmers or employees and rich outsiders or occasional employers. Never before in Loma Bonita's history have its residents had to deal with people of a higher class living in their own community.

Occasionally, I hear buyers and community members praise one another, but more frequently they use the language of opposition. For example, a lowland buyer told me that he brought his own workers up to Loma Bonita, instead of hiring community men, because "these younger workers up here want comforts without working for them." For their part, some community members express resentment of rich lowlanders who "have been deceptive about their plans for new properties" or "are slow to pay us for our work." One person commented that wealthy lowland neighbors "hardly ever even look at me directly." A few years ago, one young woman expressed a full-blown class-conscious hostility.

> Electricity is coming, but it's the *rabiblancos* [historically, members of Panama's wealthy, white oligarchy] of the *cerro* who will benefit first, not us. Maybe because we don't have money. It's not fair that those who have more than 50 years of living here yearning for electricity haven't gotten it, while those who recently arrived already do.

Tonight at dinner, sitting around the table with Esperanza and Viviana, I describe the lowlanders' houses I've seen today. Esperanza says, "At least all those people live high up in the *cerro* and leave us alone. But now there's one living down here." She's referring to a couple from the lowlands who have bought land and built a house not high up in the *cerro* but near her home. "Will they be good neighbors or enemies?" she wonders.

**BOX 5.4 A WIDER LENS: RESIDENTIAL TOURISM AND LAND GRABBING IN THE GLOBAL SOUTH AND LATIN AMERICA**

Residential tourism in Loma Bonita is still very small in scale. But in other areas of Panama (Boquete and Bocas del Toro) and other Central American countries, the prospect of spectacular profits from this type of tourism has led to a frenzy of corporate, large-scale real estate deals. With government support, wealthy foreign and domestic elites have bought, leased, or appropriated large areas of land for conversion into spaces for wealthy tourists or speculators. The documented outcome for small-scale farmers and Indigenous peoples who had been living on these lands – often, as in Loma Bonita, without legal titles – has been dispossession and/or displacement, sometimes violently. As well, this tourism process has spawned rampant land speculation, environmental damage, and a decline in food security.[13]

One way to understand this large-scale acquisition of land for residential tourism is to see it as one small part of the massive global process of "land grabbing" currently underway around the world, especially in the Global South. In recent years, powerful corporate entities (including corporations, governments and nonprofits) in the developed and richer developing countries have invested huge sums to gain control over vast tracts of land; one estimate cites 80 million hectares "grabbed" as of 2016.[14] In Latin America, including Panama, many acquisitions are being used for "flex crops" like palm oil (for food or fuel) or for fruit vineyards, tree plantations, conservation projects, or mining.[15]

Land grabbing in the South, of course, has a long history, going at least as far back as colonial times, but the current trend, say analysts, is distinguished by the enormous speed and size of land acquisitions. Some view these massive land grabs as part of a reconfiguration of global capitalism, whereby diverse powerful corporate entities respond to contemporary global crises (such as food and energy security, climate change, and financial investments) in ways they think will profit them in the long run.

The damage to people, animals, and environments that these global land grabs have brought has not gone uncontested. Around the world, the victims of land grabbing and the social movements that support these victims continue to organize to curtail or stop land acquisitions that undermine people's livelihoods, cultures, and human rights, as well as pollute and destroy the environments that support all living things. One current example is the public campaign against TIAA, the giant pension fund for retired teachers and other professionals in the United States, whose investment portfolio by 2017 had acquired almost 2 million acres of farmland around the world.[16] Blog posts, email list servers, and petition campaigns are among the tactics being used by a coalition of environmental and human rights organizations to expose violations and pressure TIAA to divest its agricultural lands in Brazil and the United States.[17]

# 6

# Next Generations: Who's Heading Home Again? (2019)

*Esperanza's dream has always been to see her children and grandchildren return to Loma Bonita and remake it into their home. Might they come back?*

## CHILDREN OF ESPERANZA AND ANDRÉS

Tony is visiting Loma Bonita from the city for a week. The presence of this white-haired, ever-playful, 65-year-old son with an imposing belly always seems to cheer Esperanza. She, Viviana, Sophia, and I sit outside around the patio table in late afternoon in excited anticipation. Tony is about to try out his $500 experiment. This morning, he had assembled the necessary pieces, all bought secondhand from acquaintances: a small electric pump, several thick electric cords, and numerous long plastic pipes. In back of the house, atop a hill in the orange grove, sits the final piece: a 50-gallon black plastic water tank. All day, he worked to set things up. He dammed the water in the stream near the house and installed the pump under the water. He attached pipes to the pump and ran them from the stream up and over a hill and into the tank.

Will it work? Tony plugs in the pump. It starts. We hear water from the stream moving through the pipes. Thirty-five minutes later, the water tank is full. He opens the tank's faucet, and water flows from tank to orange trees through other pipes he's positioned. Irrigation for the first time. We clap and cheer wildly. These orange trees are dying, and Tony hopes to save them; he'll come back to Loma Bonita for a few months, he says, to fertilize them.

Two things make this irrigation experiment possible: electricity in Loma Bonita (since 2014) and Tony's recent retirement from a 40-year urban career in construction and carpentry. Although he sometimes works on short-term contracts for his old boss, he has more time to spend with his family in Loma Bonita, as well as a monthly pension and some savings in the bank.

Viviana and Sophia still alternate three-month stays in Loma Bonita to take care of their mother, but they're here together now to help harvest and sell the family's oranges. And they've figured out how to earn a little extra money when in Loma Bonita by selling coffee to other community members. No, it's not just any ordinary coffee. They're selling a specialty powder made with the extract of a red mushroom that's billed as promoting health and curing disease by the international corporation that manufactures and distributes it worldwide. This corporation sets up specialty stores in a given country and then establishes networks of buyers and sellers, frequently women from middle and poorer classes who earn commissions, points, and titles with their sales. Last year, Lety became one of their coffee sellers and then recruited her sisters in Loma Bonita into her distribution network. A number of people in Loma Bonita buy regularly and swear by the coffee's health benefits.

~

Esperanza tells me she feels happy because her children, pictured in Figure 6.1, want to buy land in Loma Bonita; she has too few hectares of her own to accommodate them all. We're sitting on mint-green plastic chairs in her patio. With her delicate hands waving like a dancer, Esperanza relates the story of her daughter Lety's first land purchase.

> When Daniel [a neighbor] was ill and needed cash a few years ago, he put word out that he wanted to sell a plot of his orange grove land for $15,000. I knew that was way too much, that he had paid less than $5,000 for that land not long before. It's not even a hectare, and not even all good land [*callejon*]. But it did have orange and other fruit trees ready to harvest.

**Figure 6.1. Children of Esperanza and Andrés, 2016.**

So Esperanza opened negotiations with Daniel on Lety's behalf. At one point, Daniel was in Esperanza's house and the negotiations got so hot, Sophia later told me, that she had to tell him to leave – "before you give my 91-year-old mother a heart attack." In the end, the price was reduced to $10,000, and Lety was allowed to pay little by little. Esperanza supplied the down payment from her life's savings, and Lety slowly began paying back Daniel, thanks to profits from her outdoor food stall business, The Sun Comes Out for Everyone. This business also underwrote the cost of two other very small plots in Loma Bonita, bought from community men who now live with their families in the city. Lety has begun building a little house on Daniel's former land where she and her family "will enjoy the view, the breeze, nature, and the sounds of the stream and frogs." One of the smaller lots has the advantage, explains Lety, of being high up where cell-phone signals reach. "The view on that hill is spectacular, so maybe someday I'll build a cabana and conserve the land." Her teenaged son questions why she's putting her hard-earned money into this land. She just answers, "Someday you'll understand that it's for you."

Sophia has also purchased a tiny plot of a few hundred square meters for $2,500; it's got orange, mandarin, and banana trees already producing. But she won't even consider building a house on this land, she says, unless she can convince her husband to come live in Loma Bonita. "There's no use having a house that sits empty awaiting the next thief."

Son Tony, too, explored the possibility of buying a lot from relatives. But they said no because they planned to get legal title to their half-hectare lot and then sell it for much more than Tony's offer.

The price and value of land continues to rise in Loma Bonita and the region. Added to the influence of "lowlanders' purchases" is a recent increase in demand for land by community families themselves, especially those who, like Lety, Sophia, and Tony, have worked for decades in the city, have some cash on hand, and can see retirement ahead. With a paved road and electricity now available in their place of birth – and cell-phone and Wi-Fi reception on the horizon – many entertain the possibility of a full- or part-time return, or of the purchase of local land as an investment for their children. I was not surprised, therefore, to learn recently of a big change at the home of Cristino Blanco. He's the man who in 2009 (Chapter 5) was selling many lots to lowlanders because, as he then told me, his children in the city "won't be coming back to stay." But, in 2019, two are back. One has built a house on Cristino's property; the other has moved in with him and opened a small dry goods store. Both demand that he stop selling land to lowlanders.

Esperanza and her children have also decided that Esperanza should try to get legal title to her land in order to protect it from others' claims and increase its dollar value. For years, Esperanza and Andrés, like all Loma Bonita families, had waited for the government to make good on its promise to help them secure land titles cheaply. But it never happened. So two years ago, Esperanza's children gave up on the government and began the expensive, time-consuming, and bureaucratic nightmare of applying for legal title to Esperanza's lot in Frailecito. David knew what had to be done, and he and Sophia made several trips to authorities in 2017 to get necessary forms. Then they returned to the government land office in Penonomé with a battery of prepared papers, including photocopies of their *cedulas* (official identity cards), a photo of their land, a formal petition to measure it, and signed statements from all those with adjoining property attesting to the veracity of their claim. They also had to hire a government-certified land measurer as well as laborers to prepare the land for the measurer. That initial step alone cost $700, sending all five of Esperanza's children scrambling to raise their $140 contribution. It's two years later, and still no legal title has been issued. Why? In part, they say, because they've not been willing to slip someone $500 "under the table."

"Why do you want to have land in Loma Bonita?" I asked Sophia.

"I know everyone here and have beautiful memories. For me, Loma Bonita is still home."

## GRANDCHILDREN OF ESPERANZA AND ANDRÉS

What about Sophia's children and the other 11 grandchildren of Esperanza and Andrés? What's their connection to Loma Bonita? After all, none was born and raised there. They're creatures of urban Panama, with young lives so different from those of their parents and grandparents. Consider just their education.

Esperanza once told me, "The 'mind' today is like the machete of the past." She and Andrés had always understood that school, not farming, would be the door to a better future for their children, and they had struggled mightily to get all five through six grades, three years beyond what they had achieved. They succeeded, but then of necessity had to send all but David to work in urban Panama. Once in the city, their children had found it daunting to continue schooling while trying to earn a living and raise their own families there. Neither Tony nor Viviana ever found time to pursue the "mind path," but their two sisters did.

When Sophia went to work as a live-in domestic in the city, she had already attended two years of middle school in Copé, but she had had to drop out because her parents needed her financial help. It took Sophia five years working as an urban domestic to find an employer who would let her attend school, but she was allowed to go only on her day off. For three years, she took classes from 1–5 p.m. every Sunday, and she finally did get her high school diploma. Lety, too, suffered through two bosses and four years of domestic work before she found an employer who would give her permission to study sewing at night. "I'd go to school from 5 to 11 p.m. and was always so exhausted that I'd sleep standing up," she told me. Yet eventually Lety did finish middle school while working. (Twenty years later, still thirsty for education, she got her high school diploma and entered university.)

It's no surprise, given this history, that a driving force in the lives of the children of Esperanza and Andrés has been to enable their own children to aim higher, to high school and even university. Today, 9 of their 15 grandchildren have finished high school, and 2 more were only a few courses away from graduation when they chose instead to go to work.

Two of these high school graduates have gone further and earned university degrees, and a third should graduate in a few years. Viviana's youngest daughter, Janeth, is one. She began university classes after high school with money from her own earnings as a store clerk, as well as with contributions from her mother and siblings. Then life got more complicated. At age 20, Janeth had a baby and became a single parent. For a while, her mother took care of baby Omar so that Janeth could continue commuting daily from their home near Colón to Panama City, where she attended university classes after working in a day job that she enjoyed in a city park. Then life got even more complicated. In 2015, Janeth's grandfather, Andrés, had a very bad fall in Loma Bonita, and her mother and aunt Sophia decided they had to take turns living there to help out their parents. That ended Janeth's free, reliable, and loving childcare arrangement, and prompted big life changes. She explained:

> I had to bring Omar to Panama City so I could keep working. We moved into Mama's old house in El Mirador[1] where my brother and sister were living, since this was rent free. Omar was my top priority. I wanted him to go to a private school so he could get a good start to his education; public schools near El Mirador had too many students, too few teachers, and not enough different types of classes, like English. But I had a big problem – my $500-a-month salary wasn't enough to send Omar to private school.

So Janeth quit her job at the park and got work teaching at a private primary school. Although her salary was still low, Omar could attend tuition free. For the next few years, she taught in two different private schools on one-year contracts, continuing to take night classes thanks to her brother's wife who took care of her son. During school vacations, she sent Omar to Loma Bonita to be with her mother and grandparents. In 2017, a decade after she began her university studies, Janeth graduated from the University of Panama with a BA degree majoring in "tourism." But she wanted more.

> I wasn't a great student all my life, but I have this passion to keep going, and with God's help to improve myself for me and for my son. I'm not having an easy time, but in the end, I believe that all sacrifice has its rewards.

And so, soon after graduation, having gotten a new one-year teaching contract in a private school for herself and Omar, Janeth signed up for another two-year university program on weekends that would allow her eventually to teach in public as well as private schools. She wrote to me about this via WhatsApp:

> I'm in school again, this time to get a "professor" title. I go every Saturday and have five classes and lots of homework for each one. I'm feeling very stressed out with things to do, so for the moment, I'm just trying to cope with it all. Trying my best, with God's help, to do well this semester.

On Christmas day in 2017, she sent me a photo of her and Omar. The message said, "Omar and I are a small family, but one full of love."

A year later, I'm in Panama City sitting in a restaurant and awaiting Janeth who is to meet me for lunch. I see a young woman walking toward me smiling. She's wearing a colorful print blouse with off-the-shoulder sleeves, her long, curly, dark hair trailing down her back. I think, "Wow, Janeth has become a confident-looking, beautiful, 30-year-old." She has broken up with her previous boyfriend, she tells me. "He got too controlling. I feel like I'm an independent person." About school: she's just finished her last required class for her university program and has only an internship to complete before graduating. "I know your mother is proud of you – and so am I," I tell her. "It's like a chain," she says.

> Each generation tries to improve, to do better. Mama worked to give me as much education as she could within her possibilities – more than she had – and I'm trying to do the same for my son.

But for now, she's out of work again; when her annual school contract ended, there weren't enough students signed up for tourism classes for the next school year. She's just applied for a job at three other schools and a call center and, in the meantime, is earning a little money by tutoring one student and working part time as a cashier at a pharmacy.

She's excited to tell me about her dream for the future – to become an environmental engineer. More school ahead for Janeth.

Later I learn that, with help from a cousin, Janeth did get another one-year teaching job at a private school, and she and her son moved to that cousin's house to be closer to the new school. She earns $750 a month and is free from rent thanks to her cousin. And Omar gets another year of private school.

Like Janeth, most of Esperanza and Andrés's other grandchildren are employed in the city. Now in their 20s and 30s, they work in stores, construction sites, offices, supermarkets, or as traveling salespeople. One day, while Tony and I sip freshly squeezed orange juice in Esperanza's patio in Loma Bonita, he tells me how proud he is that all five of his children have a job. He goes down the list. The oldest son, born in 1976 with a disability, is packing groceries at a supermarket. Two other married sons – each with three young children – are bricklayers who, like their father, began this career as teenagers. Tony's oldest daughter, a single mother with a young son, works for a company that cleans offices, while his other daughter, Zita, has been employed for several years with a bread company. Each day, Zita leaves her three children with her mother or boyfriend and travels by foot and bus to various supermarkets in her "territory." She keeps track of bread inventories, arranges merchandise, and communicates this information to her boss on a company handheld computer. Zita has been careful to save her money, says Tony, and she recently bought a neighbor's old house that she plans to fix up and eventually rent out. He has lent her much of his savings for this project, money he had intended to spend on a used car.

To enter the home of Tony and Noris in the urbanization project where they've lived for more than two decades is like entering a small city. Four of their five children – along with their children – live there. Three have added rooms onto their parents' original house, and a fourth built his home on an adjoining lot. When they gather together for a meal, 16 people share the table. Rent is not a big budget item in this family.

None of Esperanza's grandchildren today works in the less remunerative and less prestigious jobs of live-in domestic or unskilled laborer that their grandmother and parents had filled at their ages. Like Zita, they are setting their sights on a better life, and also on one with wider vistas. The first thing Viviana's son did after making a down payment on a little red Toyota car was to take his wife, child, and mother on a two-day car trip to a town in western Panama where none had ever been before. Extending that vista even further – much further – one of Viviana's daughters now lives in Rome with a man she met on an internet dating site.

Yet, the urban working lives of these young women and men still rest on a shaky ledge. Like Janeth, most do contract work for very modest salaries with no job security; in January of 2019, three said they thought they'd be out of their jobs soon and were looking for new possibilities.

~

And Loma Bonita? What's their connection to this tiny rural community a half-day's travel away? Only a few ever lived there for more than a month, although most spent fondly remembered yearly vacations there.

Back in 2000, Viviana's 23-year-old son Sebastián told me he hoped his grandparents would never sell their land. "God doesn't want anyone other than us to come vacation on this land," he'd said. But when I asked if he would like to go live in Loma Bonita someday, he didn't hesitate:

> I love to be there with nature, the river, the fruit trees, but only for vacations. Once the rains come, I get bored and want to be back in the city where I'm accustomed to living.

His sister, Isabel, agreed, "Yes, I want to go for vacations to eat oranges, but not more. I feel alone there, as though all is silence. I'm accustomed to the noise of the city."

That was years before there was a paved road to Loma Bonita, and electricity. What about now in 2019? I asked seven others if they might want to come live in Loma Bonita someday. Almost all said they liked to visit – "to recharge my battery, rest, and relax" – but then to return to the city where there's some work, better schools for children, modern comforts, and excitement.

To my knowledge, none of Esperanza and Andrés's grandchildren has an interest in coming to live in Loma Bonita or feels a connection to Loma Bonita's land as "home." (Many of those grandchildren are pictured in Figure 6.2.) Certainly, they don't see farming in their future; most don't even know how to use a machete, except, as one told me, "to cut grass." They are wageworkers, part of Panama's insecure working

**Figure 6.2. Esperanza and many of her children, grandchildren, and great-grandchildren, 2017.**

class, who see their chain of improvement in the city. For them, it seems, the city, not Loma Bonita, is "home." Might this change in the future? Of course. Detrimental developments in the transit zone or major improvements in Loma Bonita and the interior could someday provide a strong reason to return to Loma Bonita. And right now their parents are staking claims to land there, just in case.

## LOMA BONITA 2019: FARMERS AND LABORERS

Loma Bonita is still a farming community. Able-bodied adults continue to go to their *monte* to plant yuca, beans, corn, bananas, and plantains for home consumption, and to cultivate oranges and sometimes coffee for sale in the markets. A few still raise some cattle. But no family today has enough land to grow all that its members need and want to eat or to sell enough products to meet their new desires for washing machines, refrigerators, or children's schooling. For these things and

**BOX 6.1 A WIDER LENS: PANAMA 2018 – STILL TWO UNEQUAL WORLDS**

They used enough steel to erect 29 new Eiffel Towers, and spent a decade in construction. But, finally, on June 26, 2016, the expansion of the Panama Canal was completed at a cost of more than $5 billion.[2]

Why expand the Panama Canal? As global trading grew rapidly in the 1990s, cargo ships got too big to fit through the original Panama Canal, and shipping companies began switching to the Suez Canal.[3] The expansion, they hoped, would return this commerce to Panama.

Construction took ten years due to problems with design, labor, finances, and serious criticisms about environmental issues. Nevertheless, since its opening, the expanded canal has spawned a lively business, with the United States – a staunch supporter of the project[4] – accounting for 68 percent of transits during the first 20 months.[5]

Panama's canal and other of its international services, like banking and tourism, have made the country into one of the fastest growing economies in the world; the average annual economic growth rate was 7.2 percent between 2001 and 2013[6] and 4.6 percent in the past five years.[7] But Panama's ultra-dependence on providing international services also makes it exceptionally vulnerable to global market shifts. In 2018, for example, worldwide economic downturns, trade disputes, and climatic changes affecting water levels in the Panama Canal dragged Panama's growth rate down to 3.7 percent.[8] Still, this growth rate was higher than that of most countries.

The problem is that this prosperity has not trickled down far enough. Panama is still ranked by the World Bank among the top five most unequal countries in Latin America, with almost one-fifth of its people still living in poverty.[9] Worse, a third of Panamanian children live in poverty, a figure that tragically soars to 90 percent for youth of some Indigenous groups.[10] Hardest hit are rural Panamanians, about a third of the population. The enormous wealth that has been created in Panama's transit zone for 500 years still does not flow into its interior. Half the rural population lived in poverty in 2016,[11] with rates for rural Indigenous peoples reaching as high as 93 percent in some places.[12] It's no surprise then that the contribution of agriculture to Panama's economic growth plummeted from 8 percent to 1.8 percent between 2000 and 2018.[13]

much more, every household must now find a way to access sufficient cash. And the main path to get it – just as in Andrés and Esperanza's time – is for most young family members to leave and find wage work far away where many are likely to stay to raise their own children. In 2017, for example, there were about 75 permanent households in Loma Bonita.[14] In almost half (35), all children over 16 – or all but one – were living far away either working or in school.[15] This exodus of younger men and women has left a majority of Loma Bonita homes peopled by the old and the very young.

Adults who stay are ever on the alert for additional ways to earn money. Often this is through mini-commerce, like the "health coffee" that Viviana and Sophia sell. A few mostly older people still weave and sell hats, but the scarcity and cost of materials to make them and their low profitability have greatly reduced this commerce. Tina does still weave and sell hats, but she also has a more "modern" way to earn her *reales* (literally 5¢). Walking with her in Loma Bonita is a stop-and-go journey because she's ever on the lookout for discarded cans. She retrieves and crushes them with her foot, throws them into a sack, and later delivers them to a neighbor who pays her 20¢ for 100 cans. This neighbor, in turn, resells the cans to a son-in-law from a nearby community who has a truck and takes them (along with other merchandise) to sell to a recycling dealer in Panama City.

There also are a few small-scale businesses in Loma Bonita today. Three families own trucks and buy oranges locally to take to Panama City for resale, and three others have very small dry goods stores. Another two families are trying to grow coffee commercially again with help from a government program offering fertilizers and seminars on irrigation techniques. And then there's the "beer bar," opened recently in the back of one family's house, that sends music, conversation, laughter, or anger ringing into Loma Bonita's previously quiet night.

# Concluding Thoughts

## GLANCING BACK: CONFRONTING A CENTURY OF GLOBAL CHANGE IN LOMA BONITA

It's 1922. Esperanza Ruiz is born in Loma Bonita in her grandparents' one-room adobe house with its red tile roof. Living in this house with her grandparents and mother are three aunts, an uncle, and three cousins. Loma Bonita is a place where people walk barefoot and climb down to streams to get water for bathing, washing clothes, cooking, and drinking. They use kerosene lanterns for light, cook on woodstoves, and "relieve" themselves in the forest. There's no schooling for community members, and every adult is a farmer, producing much of what a family needs to live, but little more. Most people born in Loma Bonita stay here or nearby all their lives and never get to faraway places like Panama City in the transit zone. All are poor, with few material possessions, but they're in control of decisions about how they'll spend their days, and they have relatives all around to help out. And in their *monte* there's usually plenty of yuca to eat.

Fast forward to 2019. Esperanza Ruiz is a 96-year-old widow who lives in Loma Bonita in a five-room cement-block house with a metal roof and an indoor kitchen and bathroom. Water from a community aqueduct flows through spigots in this house, and since 2014, Esperanza needs only to flick a switch to get electric light and watch TV. Cell-phone signals do not yet reach her house, but on Loma Bonita's highest hills, the world is a cell-phone call away. Yuca, corn, and beans still grow in her *monte*, but most of her food comes from a store. During harvest time, trucks pull up near her house to buy her oranges and take them down to Panama City for resale. Esperanza has been a traveler her entire adult life, moving between Loma Bonita and urban Panama to work as a live-in domestic or to help her children who live there. Her five children also left to work in the city as teenagers, but unlike their mother, they stayed in the capital to raise families; two have been employed as household domestics, one as a seamstress, and another in construction, and the fifth is a Catholic priest. As urban workers, not farmers, they have always been dependent for their sustenance on job opportunities in the transit zone.

Between these two different worlds of 1922 and 2019 lies a century of socioeconomic transformation in Loma Bonita. In this book, I've traced the slow process by which the community's production, labor, and land have been drawn into the orbit of Panama's globalized capitalist economy in the transit zone. As much as possible, I've let Esperanza and her family relate the tale of these hundred years by way of their recollections of what happened to them and how they responded. Through their eyes, we've gotten to see them as both victims and protagonists in their histories.

They've been victims in this sense: being born into poor rural families ever short on money, education, credit, and political clout set limits on their options. Yes, they could grow coffee and oranges for sale, but lacking resources to fertilize, irrigate, or transport their products left them dependent for earnings on Copé's merchants, and on the low and fluctuating prices paid for their cash crops in national and global markets. Yes, they could usually get work in cities, towns, and lowland plantations, but in jobs that were low paying, short term, dead end, and highly exploitative. Yes, they could sell land to outsiders, but at prices abysmally lower than its value in the national land market. It's true that this century of integration into the capitalist market economy has provided Esperanza and her family with many more goods, services, and comforts than her ancestors could have imagined. At the same time, their disadvantaged place as poor rural and urban workers has left them more dependent for survival on employers, merchants, politicians, and distant markets that they can't control. And they have lost the power their ancestors once had over many decisions about the use of their own production, labor, and land.

And yet their achievements against these odds are what stand out in their life stories. Their educational gains are a good example. While Esperanza's grandparents and parents had no schooling at all and Esperanza and Andrés completed only three grades, their five children surpassed them: in 2019, two had finished six grades; two, high school; and one, university. Their 15 grandchildren had done better still: nine finished high school, and two completed university.

Their stories show us how they sometimes managed to move forward despite obstacles galore. From among their limited options, we see them again and again finding small openings for action that might improve their lives. Remember 16-year-old Esperanza walking alone for 10 hours to Penonomé to escape an abusive man and head toward a possibly better future. Remember also Esperanza's mother, Natalia, braving embarrassment and repudiation in government offices to fight against that unjust land claim and assert her rights. Recall, too, when Esperanza and Andrés defied great difficulties and dangers to move to "the other side" because they saw this as their only way to access land to produce more food for their growing family. In the same vein, during the 1970s and 80s, they joined Loma Bonita's labor and food cooperatives, with the hope of improving food security for themselves and others.

Some of their efforts to seize new opportunities failed. Natalia did not win much land in the end, nor did joining Loma Bonita's cooperative groups help Esperanza and Andrés (or most others) significantly improve their material lives. On the other hand, their treks to "the other side" did provide more food for their family for a few years, and Esperanza's four-decade domestic work career paid off in the long term. With money from these jobs, she and Andrés managed to raise five children to adulthood with, at least, a sixth-grade education, and to give the world another young priest.

Above all else, their stories show that Esperanza and her family survived all these great struggles – whatever their outcome – by drawing on the one resource they each held in abundance: each other. When Esperanza was hauled into court by her cousin's ex-boyfriend or mistreated by an employer, she could count on her mother, siblings, cousins, husband, or children to be there to house, feed, and support her. In turn, when Esperanza's cousin Marcela had to escape an abusive man in Colón, Esperanza was there to assist her. When Esperanza's son David needed food, money, clothing, or school supplies during his 16-year journey to become a priest, his parents and every one of his siblings shared the burden. Just as they all did to help their sister Viviana, when she returned from Darién with three youngsters but no money, food, or housing. Just as they all did when Andrés needed help toward the end of his life, and now, Esperanza. And this cooperative approach to life's exigencies continues in the age of Esperanza's grandchildren, as when Zita could count on her father's savings to support her real estate success and when Janeth's cousin provided free rent to help her out.

Reflecting on cooperation in a gendered world, I'd like to highlight the six-decade relationship between Esperanza and Andrés. Of course, they had differences and conflicts, a few of which reached my very eyes, but what I routinely noted through the years was how complementary and flexible was their everyday division of labor; this book abounds with examples. Beyond these more visible aspects of their relationship, I saw something harder to come by: strong support for each other's life goals and decisions, and sheer pleasure at each other's successes.

Esperanza's whole family has held on to a generous spirit with one another, even when there was disagreement about decisions. No one in this family, including the generation of Esperanza's grandchildren, has yet made it into the middle class; work has never been secure or steady, and finances have always been on the edge. We can't know what opportunities may come their way in this globalized, ever-changing world – whether serious efforts will emerge to address rural and urban poverty and inequality or climate changes that threaten droughts, heat waves, and food scarcities. But we can be sure that Esperanza's descendants will be on the lookout for every possibility. And, if history serves as guide, they're likely to be there to try to catch one another from falls or help each other get up again.

At 96 years old in 2019, Esperanza was still busy thinking ahead about her family's welfare. She was encouraging her children to buy land in Loma Bonita "to make sure there's enough space for everyone, if they need to come 'home.'" When I asked her about her own future plan, she had this to say:

*Por mi parte, cuando venga Dios, estaré tranquila, lista. Ya he comido mucha yuca.*

For my part, when God comes for me, I'll be tranquil, ready. In my lifetime, I've gotten to eat lots of yuca.

## OTHER FAMILIES, SIMILAR STORIES

Had I written about a different family than Esperanza's, the details of that story would have varied. Economic factors, such as the amount and type of land and animals held by a family, influence its history. So do the number, age, and gender of children, which determine the size and capability of a family's agricultural and wage-labor force. Personal factors also play a role. Are women in the family less assertive than Esperanza or men more controlling or violent than Andrés? Does cooperation or conflict dominate a couple's life together? Do children fare better or worse than Esperanza's with regard to jobs, spouses, and education? Do they grow up to be more or less ambitious or cooperative?

All of these factors interact to shape a particular family's history and outcomes. Yet, in certain key ways, most Loma Bonita families find themselves in similar circumstances today. As I've discussed, a century-long process of global capitalism and population increase has left them with inadequate landholdings, a need for cash to meet their livelihoods, and a lack of decent wage jobs, high schools and universities, or hospitals nearby. The major solution has been for most young people to leave Loma Bonita to work and raise their families elsewhere in Panama's lowland cities, towns, and plantations. Increasingly since the 1970s, young men have joined their sisters in these migrations. Although male advantages still persist in Loma Bonita with regard to access to land and agricultural production (Chapter 3), the well-being of families today pivots less on their landholdings – which for most are small – and more on the fate of children's wage labor and faraway lives. Aging adults in almost all community households in 2019 had few or none of their children in the community to help work their fields, manage their everyday affairs and problems, and share stories at night.

This was so even in families that historically had the largest landholdings and better labor conditions for their children. One case is the family of Dionisio Ruiz and Belsi Ortiz whose land advantages (and strong bias for male dominance) enabled their six sons (though not their seven daughters) to stay in Loma Bonita after marriage. Together, these six sons raised 37 children in the community, but by 2017, only 6 still lived and farmed there.

This means that, whatever the specifics of their situations, almost all Loma Bonita families today face predicaments like those that Esperanza and Andrés had to confront: how to deal with serious labor and cash shortages, the dependence on help from faraway children, and the care of young and old family members.

## ESPERANZA, HER FAMILY, AND ME, 2019

Sometime in the 1990s, I was standing outside a store in Copé with Andrés when an acquaintance of his whom I didn't know came up to talk with him, an obviously quizzical look on his face about who I was. Andrés greeted him and introduced me as his daughter. I'll never forget the stunned look on that man's face until he realized it was said in jest. Since then, though, slowly this joke has taken hold as part-joke, part-truth. In only part-jest, I'll sometimes call Esperanza "mama," and all five of her children and I will call one another brother or sister.

The half-truth is heartfelt by all involved. Over the years, I've visited and slept in their homes in the city; observed their work sites; celebrated births, birthdays, and new jobs; and commiserated about the sick children, unemployment, abusive men, and alcoholism in their lives. My family, especially my son and later his wife and two daughters, has spent time with them in Loma Bonita and the city. More recently, the electronic age has kept us in touch when I'm not in Panama. It used to take up to six weeks to move a letter between us, but I learned of Andrés's death within hours via a WhatsApp message from David. And sometimes now, when I'm in Pittsburgh and have a question for one of them, I get on my computer instead of an airplane to get the answer.

While my longtime fieldwork has enabled Esperanza, her family, and me to form openhearted ties, these connections do differ from other close relationships. I am, after all, always the anthropologist, pulling

**Figure C.1. Esperanza and Gloria, working together, sharing lives, 2017. Photo by Hans Buechler.**

my notebook out of my backpack to record what they say and do. As well, the inequality between our lives persists; while I visit them with money from grants or my small bank account, they cannot afford to visit me in the United States. Nevertheless, our deep feelings for one another show the power of shared humanity to transcend the global pecking order. (Figure C.1 shows Esperanza and Gloria working together and sharing their lives.) One day in 2019, Esperanza and I were discussing the many things I had learned from her over the years. It occurred to me to ask her if she had learned anything from me. Without pause, she said, "You're someone who thinks everyone is equal; I never knew that was possible before."

## LIFE NARRATIVES AND LONG-TERM PARTICIPANT OBSERVATION RESEARCH

In the introduction, I made claim to taking a unique approach in this life narrative about Esperanza Ruiz and her family. Instead of learning about Esperanza's history through the traditional life history interview method that asked her to think back and remember her life, I reconstructed her life story by drawing on my five decades of research in Loma Bonita. I suggested three advantages to using this alternative method. Now that Esperanza's story has been told, I can illustrate each of them with examples from her life.

The first advantage I proposed was that the use of information from long-term research rather than retrospective interviews alone improves the chance of understanding how Esperanza experienced events back at the time they were happening. Take, as one example, her involvement in 1972 in the Torrijos military government's effort to organize the country for an election of a representative to a new national assembly (Chapter 4).

I was in the community that whole year, documenting the fate of this political reform. Because I was there, writing in my fieldnotes everything I learned from and about Esperanza, I could include in this book the story of that first organizing meeting in Loma Bonita's school, with its sham election that catapulted Esperanza involuntarily into the political world as president of a women's committee. I was with her after that school gathering when she initiated a private meeting with the *regidor*, Sr. Cristo, to admit her confusion about the government's motives and plans. And I was also by her side following that meeting as she climbed back home with a handful of trusted community members. All expressed confusion, worry, and fear about the military government, and all agreed with Esperanza when she warned of the danger of noncompliance. A few weeks later, I was with Esperanza at her house when Juana, a member of her women's committee, came to ask advice about family problems she was having because of her political work. I listened as Esperanza empathized with the political situation facing Juana and other women and described her own evolving ideas about new political actions that she thought could benefit both women and men in Loma Bonita.

If interviewed today, would Esperanza remember these details of events and feelings that happened 50 years ago? That she felt political fear and confusion? That she showed political courage, savvy, and leadership as well as a consciousness of women's problems? Little chance of this, I'd argue. To the contrary, her later recollections to me about "those days" have centered on how her women's committee was disbanded after the election, with lots of hard feelings all around. But I had been there in 1972, committing those moments of Esperanza's life, and of community history, into the written record.

The second advantage of using long-term field research rather than retrospective interviews alone, an advantage also mentioned in the introduction, is that I could capture Esperanza moving through life *not* just as an individual but as part of a four-generational family whose members had complex and emotional ties. The decade-long saga of her mother's decline and death illustrates the importance of this broader vista (Chapter 5). During five visits to Loma Bonita during the 1990s, I kept track of Esperanza's difficult journey with her mother. At first, as Natalia's physical and mental health became problematic, Esperanza and her siblings agreed to take turns caring for their mother in their homes. When that arrangement fell apart, Andrés stepped up to the plate. "Bring her here," he had said. "What we eat, she will too." Because at that time Esperanza and Andrés were also taking turns going to the city to help daughters Viviana and Lety with childcare, Natalia was simply brought along to be cared for in the capital. Twice during those years, Esperanza and Andrés heeded Natalia's pleas to bring her back home to Loma Bonita, but both times ended in disaster; once, she was caught lighting matches during the night, and the other time, she had a hard fall. With Esperanza and Andrés by then almost 80, their children entered more fully into the health care fray; Lety and Viviana brought Natalia to live with them in Panama City, while Tony, Sophia, and David aided as they could. Esperanza, too, spent about two weeks a month in the city at that time, helping out with her mother's care. Etched in my mind's eye as well as in my fieldnotes was that small patio space between the houses of Lety and Viviana, crowded with table, chairs, sewing machine, and a small bed for Natalia's daytime naps. That scene said it all: life for that whole family – all three generations – revolved around Natalia's care.

I was in Panama from mid-1999 through Natalia's death in mid-2001, and my fieldnotes and memories attest to Esperanza as the central figure in her mother's care. But she was never alone. Her husband, children, and older grandchildren – and sometimes her siblings and close cousins – formed a circle around her to help care for Natalia, a three-generational embrace of support, assistance, and the pooling of scarce resources. If interviewed today, would Esperanza remember to mention the whole cast of characters who were vital to this difficult drama of responsibility and love? I think not. But I had been there numerous times, visiting Natalia and everyone involved in her care, my notebook and pen at the ready.

The third advantage to basing Esperanza's life narrative on long-term research is that it enabled me to capture the smallest details of a particular story through time and, in the process, uncover patterns and connections not easily visible using the traditional life history interview method. The involvement of Esperanza and her family in rural-urban migration provides a case in point.

Over the years, I've gathered detailed migration histories from Esperanza and each of her children. Story after story shows them crisscrossing rural and urban space – moving resources, labor, ideas, information, feelings, assistance, and conflicts back and forth in both directions as a means to help themselves and each other survive and thrive. Recall, for example, that when Andrés became very sick in the 1980s (Chapter 4), Tony came from the city to Loma Bonita to take his father back to the capital where he and Lety could get him to a doctor. In the meantime, Viviana and her young children moved from Panama City to Loma Bonita for a while to help Esperanza with the harvest. Similarly, when David needed a typewriter for his studies in Penonomé (Chapter 4), Esperanza informed her children in the capital, Tony found a typewriter, and Andrés went to pick it up in Panama City, delivering it to David in Penonomé.

What is revealed in the cumulative minutiae of these stories? The dense strands of connection that this family has woven between rural and urban places. You could say that they've forged a new form of family that spans and links rural and urban space. In the course of these movements, they've remade what had been two divergent realities during Esperanza's youth – the rural and the urban – into one single social world. If Esperanza had been remembering her story of rural-urban migration today, she certainly would have exposed the importance of rural-urban connections. But it takes insights gleaned from the detailed migration experiences of her whole family to grasp the magnitude of the transformation that has taken place in both family life and the rural-urban landscape. Long-term participant observation research is up to this task.

## AFTERLIFE

Now that this book has been written, I get to ponder its afterlife. "Afterlife" is the word used by anthropologist Alisse Waterston[1] to describe her attempts to share with a wider public the ideas from her book about her father's life and worldwide violence in the twentieth century. Through presentations to a variety of academic and nonacademic audiences, Waterston hoped to stimulate a new way to think about the painful histories and circumstances of others, especially those "others" who are considered by many to be unworthy and invisible.

Like Waterston, I've tried over the years to forge an afterlife for my work – to share the results of my research both with a wider public outside of Loma Bonita and, especially, within the community itself. My "wider public" has mostly been in the capital, Panama City, where over the years I've presented my research findings in written editorials for newspapers; in presentations for nonprofits, museums, and universities; and on an occasional TV or radio show. In all of these venues, I've tried to put a face on rural and urban poverty, describe how Loma Bonita's people live and struggle, and place causation where it belongs: on capitalist development and government policies. Some of these efforts went well, some not, but all had one thing in common: they were what anthropologist Robert Borofsky[2] refers to as "one-off events" or "momentary bursts of enthusiasm." These are well meaning but not likely enduring efforts at public outreach, as I had no way to follow up on their impact.

In Loma Bonita, of course, I've hoped for a more long-lasting afterlife, but the process of sharing my work with community members has never been easy.[3] Just to get written copies of my publications to community members has required getting them translated into Spanish and then traipsing up and down slopes to deliver a copy to each household personally. Because many older community members haven't been able to read easily, I've also tried other routes. For example, I once convened a gathering (*convivencia*) to discuss one aspect of my research – the failure of outside "development projects" to improve things for most community families. It took countless hours to organize, advertise, and pull off this *convivencia*, which in the end was well attended and a fun event. But the discussion about "development" involved too few voices.

This is not to say that I've had no encouraging afterlife moments in Loma Bonita. After my first book was published in Spanish in Panama in 2001, I "returned" a copy to each community family and worked with the director of a small museum in Penonomé to organize a public presentation in that town. I secured a transportation grant that paid for chartered buses to take two people from every Loma Bonita family to the presentation, and the museum director provided them with a hot meal. There were 110 people from Loma Bonita who packed the room the day of the presentation, many of whom had helped organize the event. Some had taken charge of bus transportation; others were in the program. Loma Bonita's adorable school chorus opened with song, a group of community adults sang and danced *tamborito*, and Father David was one of the speakers on stage. In that audience, too, were many people from Penonomé and faraway Panama City. Comments from numerous community members after the event were heartening. "People from the town got to see us differently, as important people," remarked one person. And another: "To see so many people interested in this book surprised me and makes me proud to have grown up here."

Many anthropologists today struggle with the issue of an afterlife for their work. Like me, they want others, especially those who've been a part of their research, to be able to benefit in some way from it. There's a range of responses to this dilemma, depending on the anthropologist's personal and political views as well as the conditions of their fieldwork. Some design their research specifically to help bring material or political resources to those with whom they live or to provide outright support for people's political mobilizations and struggles against exploitation and repression. Others argue that to accomplish some or all of the aforementioned goals requires changing the research process itself to include those who are studied as collaborating partners in deciding what research questions to pursue and how to carry it out, analyze it, and share the results.[4] I find merit in all these research paths and have made efforts to follow some of their ideas.

My hope is to make a small contribution to our cumulative knowledge and understanding of one of the most tragic of global problems: the poverty and inequality that batters much of humankind.[5] My wish for this book is that it will have an eventful afterlife because it tells this story through the lives of real people and makes visible not only their perils and problems but also their persistence, creativity, humor, and warmth.

~

At this moment, what I most feel for the families of Loma Bonita is fear, fear that their dreams will be seriously impacted by the COVID-19 pandemic. We can't know yet how it will end, but we see that this pandemic, like many other communicable diseases and health-related problems, leads especially to the doors of people like those in Loma Bonita – the poor families of this planet. They live in close quarters, often without adequate water supplies, which means they can't social distance or wash hands frequently. If they have work, it's usually in low-paid but "essential" jobs that require their daily presence in dangerous places, like hospitals and restaurants. As I write, in November 2020, Panama's death rate (per 100,000 population) from COVID-19 is the highest in Central America and ninth highest in Latin America.[6] As I write, I know of more than a handful of diagnosed cases of the virus among people from Loma Bonita, and two deaths; one of those who died was a close relative of Esperanza's.

## LOOKING AHEAD: GLOBALIZATION AND GLOBAL CITIZENS

Since the 1990s, with help from new technologies, the globalization of capitalism has been on a tear; capital, people, goods, information, and images have been moving around the globe with unprecedented speed and scale. The lives, economies, and cultures of billions of people have been affected by and linked into this worldwide system. Big winners and losers have emerged. On the one hand, unparalleled corporate profits have made the rich much richer. On the other, failure to share this wealth with a huge slice of humanity has brought economic inequality to new heights. The World Bank reported that in 2018, half of the planet's 7.7 billion people lived on less than $5.50 a day,[7] while the richest 1 percent of people owned 45 percent of the world's wealth.[8] The COVID-19 pandemic today is only deepening this divide.

The impacts of this intensification of globalization are felt directly in Loma Bonita – for good and for bad. To the good so far, access to cell-phone and internet communication is helping family members stay in closer touch across space, even across oceans for two families that have daughters now living in Europe with men they met on internet dating sites. In another family, though, global economics and politics have brought unemployment. In 2018, Nathan Ortiz lost his job as a community development worker for an international nonprofit organization that had an office near Loma Bonita. For Nathan, there was no hiding the global connection between the US White House and his small cement-block home high on a hill in Loma Bonita.

> Trump's anti-globalization policies led donors to my organization in the United States to decrease their contributions and forced the organization's Washington office to restrict funding for its branch in Panama City. That brought staff cuts to my office here in Coclé, just when I was hoping to build an indoor bathroom in my house. So my family suffers from US policies just like you up there.

In Loma Bonita, the struggle goes on, albeit paralyzed at this moment by the pandemic. In the context of an increasingly globalized and unequal world, community members still search for ways to put food on the table, educate children, and look for small openings that might someday lead to a path toward middle-class comforts and aspirations. For readers of this book, it's my hope that your acquaintance with Esperanza and her community will encourage you to forge a life as a global citizen. By this term, I mean a person committed to being actively engaged in reshaping the world in ways that can provide more equal opportunities and benefits for everyone. To become a global citizen begins with learning about the ways that global capitalism works to give advantages to some, but not others. Global citizens apply this understanding to decisions about their own lives; they care about the injustices they come to see and want to counter them. Then, they take some action on this front – big or small; alone or, even better, with others – in their neighborhoods, cities, or countries, or in a faraway place like Loma Bonita. To take a stand anywhere in this interconnected world can reverberate widely.

I used to think that hope was the most powerful human life force, but I've changed my mind. After a half-century of conversation with Esperanza Ruiz, her family, and the people of Loma Bonita, I think it's love.

**Figure C.2. Esperanza, 2015.**

# Notes

## Introductions

1 I have been fortunate to receive partial or full funding for some of my subsequent fieldwork in Panama from various sources (see the acknowledgments), and I have personally funded other field trips through my teaching in the United States or Panama.

2 In addition to participant observation in Loma Bonita, I've learned from interviewing relevant individuals outside the community, including teachers, priests, merchants, social scientists, employers, and government officials. Among the relatively few written sources available about Loma Bonita are family documents and government records, such as land archives, maps, and agricultural surveys. For more about my research methods, see Rudolf (1999, 15–17, 221–8; 2000, 41–4, 393–405).

3 Wolf (1992, 6, 13) argues for this point of view.

4 Waterston (2019, 9).

5 I capitalize the word *Indigenous* throughout as equivalent to *American* or *Canadian*.

6 Radin was a student at Columbia University of the famous US anthropologist Franz Boas, who also widely influenced early Canadian anthropology. When the Geological Survey of Canada established a Division of Anthropology for the first time in 1910, another of Boas's students, Edward Sapir, was hired as its first chief ethnologist. Boas and a number of his students studied the Inuit and Indigenous peoples on Canada's Northwest Coast (Preston and Tremblay 2006).

7 I calculate that, of almost 600 autobiographical narratives of "North American Indians" referenced by Brumble in 1981 (a good many of them

edited by anthropologists), only about 50 were of Indigenous women (Brumble 1981).

8 Lurie (1961, 100–2, 112–3).

9 Underhill (1961, viii).

10 Frank (1995); Reed-Danahay (1997, 1).

11 On this point, see Brettell (1997, 225), Castaneda (2009), Ellis, Adams, and Bochner (2011, 273–4), Okely (1992), and Reed-Danahay (1997, 1, 2, 125).

12 Burgos-Debray (1984, xv). This autobiography (also categorized as a "testimonial" because of its intention to expose governmental repression) generated an enormous controversy within academia. For one thorough review of this debate with a favorable view toward Menchú, see Grandin (2010).

13 Behar (1993).

14 Buechler and Buechler (1996).

15 Other excellent life histories of women outside of Latin America during these years include Abu-Lughod (1993), Brettell (1982), Gmelch (1991), and Shostak (1981). For life histories of Latin American men, see Mintz (1974) and Nash (1992), and outside the region, see Crappanzano (1980). Among important earlier work applying the life history approach to studying Latin American families is Oscar Lewis (1961,1966).

16 On autoethnography see Brettell (1997), Ellis et al. (2011), Reed-Danahay (1997), and Waterston (2019, 12–13).

17 Waterston (2005, 2019).

18 Among anthropologists doing life history work, there's wide variation with regard to the number of interviews given, the setting, and the time taken, but most typically, they involve relatively short periods of time. The Buechlers interviewed Sofía Velasquez during six field visits spanning 30 years, but this is rare.

19 There are also important differences in the manner and degree to which anthropologists edit and rearrange the life narrative material for publication (Brettell 1997, 224–6; Frank 1979).

### 1. The Isthmus of Panama: Two Different Worlds (pre-1920s)

1 Estimates of this date currently vary widely, with some scientists arguing that it should be closer to 3 million years ago (Arnold, 2017; O'Dea et al., 2016).

2 Sources for archaeological information come from personal communications with Tony Ranere and Richard Cooke as well as from their publications, including Cooke (1976, 2005), Cooke and Ranere (1992a, 1992b), Cooke and Sánchez Herrera (2004), and Ranere (2006).

3 Gjording (1991, 263). Estimates of the population at the time of the Spanish invasion vary widely from 225,000 to 2 million (Jaén Suárez 1978, 50).

4 Müller-Schwarze (2015, 64–73) describes both Spanish cruelty and Indigenous armed resistance in the region of northern Coclé Province in central Panama.
5 Urracá's image is on the Panamanian one-cent coin.
6 Castillero Calvo (1995, 40–1, chap. 1).
7 The impact of the Spanish Conquest was not uniform throughout the isthmus; there were less populated areas that were less devastated than the lowlands of central Panama, as well as areas where the entire population disappeared (Castillero Calvo 1995; Richard Cooke, personal communication).
8 Wikipedia (2011).
9 Castillero Calvo (1995, 104–5). For the Spanish colonial period in Panama, see Araúz (2007) and Castillero Calvo (1995, 2015).
10 For an explanation of the term "interior," see Castillero Calvo (1971, 70–1) and Jaén Suárez (1978, 70–4).
11 Weil et al. (1972, 273). Even in the 1970s, 88–90 percent of the country's surface was still owned by the government.
12 Castillero Calvo (2015, 110); Manduley (1980, 57).
13 Zimbalist and Weeks (1991, 21).
14 Jaén Suárez (1971, 70–5, 79–80).
15 My best assessment is that this move took place in the 1830s or 1840s.
16 In the course of the nineteenth century, this state underwent several political and administrative reorganizations and was in different periods called Gran Colombia, New Granada, and, after 1886, the Republic of Colombia (Weil et al. 1972, 20–7).
17 Lasso (2019, 28–31). Important sources on Panama's Colombian period during the nineteenth century include Aparicio (2014), Araúz and Pizzurno Gelós (1993), Figueroa Navarro (1982), and Jaén Suárez (1971). Studies that discuss the Indigenous population in the mountains of Coclé during this period (and earlier) include Camargo Ríos (2002), Castillero Calvo (1995), Joly (1984), and Müller-Schwarze (2015).
18 Although Panama's merchant class continued to hold political power in the isthmus during this period, its members lacked the capital to undertake large construction projects and, therefore, pursued foreign capital, especially from the United States (Carse 2014, 78).
19 Although the railroad did open the door for the first time to certain parts of the interior, and later to large-scale commercial agriculture in banana production, this access was exclusively foreign controlled (Zimbalist and Weeks 1991, 6).
20 For analysis of the interplay between Panamanian nationalism and US imperialism, see Aparicio (2014).
21 Zimbalist and Weeks (1991, 12). Lasso (2019, chap. 1) describes a more complex picture from the perspective of Panamanian elites.
22 Carse (2014); Lasso (2019).

23 Conniff (1985).
24 Carse (2014, 173); Farnsworth and McKenney (1983, 21–2, 24).
25 After independence in 1903, Panama adopted its own currency, the "balboa," a coin that was pegged to the US dollar. In practice, however, it's been the US paper dollar that has legally circulated ever since and been used in daily transactions. Panama does not print any paper money.
26 Zindar (1988, 33).
27 Rosas Quirós (1972, 56–7). They envisioned that this road would eventually be part of a national road system running west from the capital to the Costa Rican border.

**2. Childhood: As Soon as I Opened My Eyes (1920s–1930s)**

1 Learning about Esperanza's childhood and Loma Bonita's history during the 1920s and 30s was challenging. I wasn't there, nor were there written records about the community or its people for those decades. Therefore, as I pursued this information during the 1970s, I depended heavily on the recollections and genealogies of about a dozen elder community members who had been, at least, teenagers by 1920. Some of their children, too, were important history tellers, recounting the stories their parents had told them about the "old days" and about their own early lives.
2 Rudolf (1999, 57; 2000, 109). My family genealogies show that between 1860 and 1919, over one-third (36 percent) of the women in Loma Bonita who agreed to settle down with a man for the first time already had children with other men with whom they had never lived.
3 Carse (2014, 80), Castillero Calvo (1995, chaps. 1 and 2), Conniff (1985), Priestley (1986, 6), and Zimbalist and Weeks (1991, 8).
4 Perego et al. (2012); Cooke (2015). See also Arias et al. (1992, 1) for an earlier genetic study of physical diversity in a region near Loma Bonita.
5 Weil et al. (1972, 274).
6 Rudolf (1999, 43–4; 2000, 85). Note that all currency is expressed in US dollars unless otherwise indicated.

**3. Youth: I Could Always Quit and Go Home (1940s–1950s)**

1 By my calculations, a community household needed access to use rights to about 27 hectares (almost 68 acres) to meet most subsistence needs over the long term (Rudolf 1999, 46; 2000, 87–8). In 1920, all Loma Bonita families could claim rights to this amount of land, but by 1940, 7 of 16 households could not (Rudolf 1999, 68; 2000, 135).
2 For more details, see Rudolf (1999, 66–8; 2000, 134–6).
3 Rudolf Frazier (1976, 147–9).
4 Rudolf Frazier (1976, 150, chap. 4); Rudolf (1999; 2000, chap. 5).
5 Rudolf Frazier (1976, 91); Rudolf (1999, 249n12; 2000, 436n12).
6 Rudolf (1999, 36; 2000, 119–20).

7 Rudolf Frazier (1976, 19).
8 Rudolf (1999, 235n27; 2000, 416n27).
9 Rudolf Frazier (1976, 9–10).
10 Rudolf (1983, 142; 1992; 1999, 74; 2000, 145). Similar descriptions of women's temporary pattern of rural-urban migration in other Latin American countries include Bunster and Chaney (1985), Chaney and Garcia Castro (1989), Rubbo and Taussig (1978), and Smith (1973).
11 Rudolf (2003, 143–4).

**4. Adult: A Voice Meant to Be Heard (1960s–1980s)**

1 Gjording (1991, 23).
2 LaFeber (1979, 133).
3 Rudolf (1999, 70, table 3.3; 2000, 139, table 3.3).
4 During the 1960s, Panama's sugar exports increased by almost 30 percent (Zimbalist and Weeks 1991, 29), as did work opportunities for men in the sugarcane fields of Coclé Province.
5 Rudolf (1999, 107, table 5.1; 2000, 203, table 5.1).
6 Priestley (1986, 21). Panama's traditional oligarchy by 1968 was comprised mainly of 20 families that controlled 99 of the top 120 companies (Gandásegui 1974, 151–68, cited in Gjording 1991, 266n15).
7 Zimbalist and Weeks (1991, 24–5); Manduley (1980, 62–4).
8 Zimbalist and Weeks (1991, 27, 29).
9 LaFeber (1979, 150–1).
10 Priestley (1986, 23–4).
11 Priestley (1986, 28–32); Zimbalist and Weeks (1991, 30–46).
12 Gjording (1991, 30).
13 Manduley (1980, 65).
14 Priestley (1986, 68); Zimbalist and Weeks (1991, 122).
15 Zimbalist and Weeks (1991, 122–3, 126).
16 Rudolf (1999, chap. 6; 2000, chap. 6).
17 Opazo Bernales (1988, 35–7, 124–31).
18 For details on this movement in Loma Bonita and Latin America, see Rudolf (1999, chap. 8; 2000, chap. 8).
19 Zimbalist and Weeks (1991, 128–35).
20 Scranton (1991, 85).
21 Zimbalist and Weeks (1991, 198n46, 149–50).
22 The treaties stipulated that the United States could not go against Panamanian sovereignty.
23 Leis (1999, A10).
24 Accounts of the US invasion include Buckley (1991), Gandásegui and Priestley (1990), Independent Commission of Inquiry (1991), Koster and Sánchez (1990), and Ricord (1991).
25 Zimbalist and Weeks (1991, 143–4); Scranton (1991, 69–70).
26 AFP (2018).

### 5. Elder: Doors Open, Doors Close (1990s–2019)

1 Endara had been elected president in 1989, but Noriega had annulled the election and installed his own candidate.
2 World Bank (1999).
3 Kovaleski (1999, A01).
4 Rudolf (2014, 94–6).
5 The US Peace Corps was kicked out of Panama by Torrijos in 1971, but it returned in 1990 after the US invasion.
6 *New York Times* (2012, 2019).
7 Robinson (2012).
8 Rudolf (2014, 91–3).
9 McWatters (2009, 78–9); Mellado (2011); Spalding (2013, 74).
10 CentralAmericaData (2014).
11 Rudolf (2014, 101–4).
12 The age was later lowered to 65, and the benefit raised to $120.
13 Cañada (2010); Gascón and Ojeda (2014).
14 Fairbairn (2020, 3–4).
15 Important sources on global land grabbing (or "land rushing") in Latin America include Borras Jr. et al. (2012), Edelman et al. (2018), and Fairbairn (2020).
16 Fairbairn (2020, 5).
17 Another contemporary effort is aimed at defending the land rights of the Maya of Guatemala against US-based archaeologists and their allies in the US Senate who have proposed to privatize some land within the important Maya cultural site of the Mirador-Calakmul Basin. As of July 2020, a petition against this move had over 200,000 signatures (Nazario and Cherofsky 2020).

### 6. Next Generations: Who's Heading Home Again? (2019)

1 In 2018, El Mirador was among those sectors of Panama City with the "most criminal events" (Diaz 2018).
2 Mufson (2016).
3 Kahn (2016).
4 Guevara Mann (2011).
5 Sharma (2018). China, in second place, accounted for only 18 percent.
6 World Bank (2018).
7 World Bank (2020).
8 Vega Loo (2019).
9 UNICEF (2017, 1).
10 Freire (2019).
11 Lasso (2016).
12 UNICEF (2017, 1).

13 Embassy of the Kingdom of the Netherlands in Panama (2018); Vega Loo (2019).
14 Also, Loma Bonita had about two dozen "empty houses" belonging to migrants or lowlanders.
15 In 22 of these 35 homes, the adults were over 70 years old.

### Concluding Thoughts

1 Waterston (2019, 16).
2 Borofsky (2019, 132–3, 141–2) argues that enduring work is best accomplished by collaborating with socially constituted groups that are respected by most research subjects.
3 Waterston (2019, 16) also reported a long list of "constraints" on her efforts, including the time and cost required to arrange and schedule events, create marketing materials, do advertising, travel, and provide inexpensive copies of her book.
4 Borofsky (2019, 163). See Rudolf (1999, 225, 268; 2000, 400–1, 465) for discussion of some of these alternatives. Recent work in Panama that falls under the rubric of engaged anthropology or participatory action research includes Theodossopoulos (2015), Velasquez Runk (2014), and Rodríquez Blanco and Herrera (forthcoming).
5 Borofsky (2019: 91, 132, 218) also expresses these ideas.
6 Wikipedia (2020).
7 Lardieri (2018). A quarter of humanity lived on less than $3.20 a day.
8 Credit Suisse (2018).

# Glossary

**arrowroot** A tuberous root plant, like yuca and yams.

***bollos*** Corn buns, a favorite food. These are made by grinding corn kernels, stuffing them into a corn husk, and boiling them.

***cerro*** Highest area of a mountain slope, less forested and usually not farmed, where lowlanders are buying land in Loma Bonita for houses or investment.

***chola*** Derogatory term used by lowlanders to refer to Indigenous people and poor highlanders.

***comadre*** A term meaning "co-mother." A *comadre* is one of the important relationships established by the Roman Catholic Church during baptism, confirmation, and marriage when a godmother (*madrina*) and godfather (*padrino*) are named to be a person's spiritual parents. The godparents and parents of that child also establish a lifelong relationship of mutual respect and assistance, and they refer to one another as *comadre* (co-mother) or *compadre* (co-father).

**El Mirador** Urbanization project on the outskirts of Panama City where Lety, Viviana, and now Viviana's children live.

**Frailecito** A place about a two-hour walk south of Loma Bonita where Esperanza's parents, and later Esperanza and Andrés, built a second residence.

*gringa/gringo* Someone who is a foreigner in Spain or Latin America. In Panama, the term is often used pejoratively to refer to someone from the United States.

**interior** All of Panama outside of the "transit zone." This area is mostly rural with small towns.

*junta* Cooperative labor group; important for survival in the past in Loma Bonita.

*monte* Forest land used to plant food crops.

**oligarch** Member of a small group of people having control of a country, organization, or institution.

**Penonomé** Lowland town and capital of Coclé Province. The town is a place to buy supplies, engage in small-scale trading, or access transportation for people of Loma Bonita.

**plantain** Fruit similar to a banana (same genus) but usually eaten cooked.

*pollera* Large gathered skirt with blouse worn by women for festive and important occasions.

*regidor* Local-level government official.

**subsistence** The state of working to produce what is mainly for one's use – to consume, to live. Any surplus produced doesn't accumulate and transform the system.

*tamborito* Popular folk music in Panama's countryside, featuring singing, clapping, and dancing to the beat of drums.

**transit zone** Narrow area in the center of the Isthmus of Panama where the Pacific and Atlantic oceans have been connected for centuries – first by road (sixteenth century), then railroad (nineteenth century), and then canal (twentieth century). The transit zone has become Panama's center of wealth and power with a major city at each end.

**yuca** Root of the cassava plant; similar in size and shape to a yam or sweet potato but with a bark-like skin. The yuca is a major crop for poor Panamanians because it is drought resistant, grows in poor soils, and can remain in the ground for several years until needed.

# Bibliography


Abu-Lughod, Lila. 1993. *Writing Women's Worlds: Bedouin Stories*. Berkeley: University of California Press.

AFP (Agence France-Presse). 2018. "Rights Group Calls for US Reparations over 1989 Panama Invasion." *France 24*, November 17, 2018. Accessed August 19, 2019. https://www.france24.com/en/20181117-rights-group-calls-us-reparations-over-1989-panama-invasion.

Aparicio, Fernando. 2014. "La independencia de Panamá de Colombia: entre el nacionalismo y el imperialismo." In *Panamá: Historia contemporánea*, edited by Alfredo Castillero Calvo, 146–61. Spain: Mapfre/Taurus.

Araúz, Celestino Andrés. 2007. *Bocas del Toro y el Caribe occidental: Periferia y marginalidad, siglos XVI–XIX*. Panamá: Instituto Nacional de Cultura, Editorial Mariano Arosemena.

Araúz, Celestino Andrés, and Patricia Pizzurno Gelós. 1993. *El Panamá Colombiano (1821–1903)*. Colombia: Primer Banco de Ahorros y Diario La Prensa Panamá.

Arias, Tomás, Ramiro Barrantes, Lucía Jorge, María Carles, and Jorge Azofeifa, with Richard Cooke. 1992. "Estudio sobre los 'cholos de Coclé': Determinación de su mezcla racial y orígenes genéticos." *Revista Médica de Panamá* 7, no. 3: 180–7.

Arnold, Carrie. 2017. "Hot Dispute Emerges over First Land Bridge from North to South America." *Scientific American*, February 21, 2017. Accessed January 30, 2020. https://www.scientificamerican.com/article/hot-dispute-emerges-over-first-land-bridge-from-north-to-south-america/.

Behar, Ruth. 1993. *Translated Woman*. Boston: Beacon Press.

Belli, Gioconda. 2002. *The Country under My Skin: A Memoir of Love and War.* New York: Alfred A. Knopf.

Borofsky, Robert. 2019. *An Anthropology of Anthropology.* Kailua, Hawaii: Center for a Public Anthropology.

Borras, Saturnino M., Jr., Jennifer C. Franco, Sergio Gómez, Cristóbal Kay, and Max Spoor. 2012. "Land Grabbing in Latin America and the Caribbean." *Journal of Peasant Studies* 39 (3–4): 845–72. https://doi.org/10.1080/03066150.2012.679931.

Brettell, Caroline B. 1982. *We Have Already Cried Many Tears: The Stories of Three Portuguese Migrant Women.* Cambridge: Schenkman Press.

———. 1997. "Blurred Genres and Blended Voices: Life History, History, Biography, Autobiography, and the Auto/Ethnography of Women's Lives." In *Auto/Ethnography Rewriting the Self and the Social*, edited by Deborah E. Reed-Danahay, 223–46. Oxford: Berg.

Brumble, H. David, III. 1981. *American Indian and Eskimo Autobiographies.* Lincoln: University of Nebraska Press.

Buckley, Kevin. 1991. *Panama – The Whole Story.* New York: Simon & Schuster.

Buechler, Hans C., and Judith-Maria Buechler. 1996. *The World of Sofia Velasquez: The Autobiography of a Bolivian Market Vendor.* New York: Columbian University Press.

Bunster, Ximena, and Elsa Chaney. 1985. *Sellers and Servants: Working Women in Lima, Peru.* New York: Praeger.

Burgos-Debray, Elizabeth. 1984. *I Rigoberta Menchú, An Indian Woman in Guatemala.* New York: Verso.

Camargo Ríos, Marcela. 2002. *Producción y comercio en la sociedad rural de Penonomé durante los primeros cincuenta años de la república.* Panamá: Universidad de Panamá.

Cañada, Ernest. 2010. *Tourism in Central America: Social Conflict in a New Setting.* Studies in Contrast No. 1. Barcelona: Alba Sud. http://www.albasud.org/publ/docs/32.en.pdf.

Carse, Ashley. 2014. *Beyond the Big Ditch – Politics, Ecology, and Infrastructure at the Panama Canal.* Cambridge, MA: The MIT Press.

Castaneda, Terri. 2009. "American Indian Lives and Voices: The Promise and Problematics of Life Narratives." *Reviews in Anthropology* 38: 132–65. https://doi.org/10.1080/00938150902889724.

Castillero Calvo, Alfredo. 1971. *La fundación de la Villa de Los Santos y los orígenes históricos de Azuero.* Panama City, Panamá: Editorial Litografica, Edición de la Dirección Nacional de Cultura, Ministerio de Educación.

———. 1995. *Conquista, evangelización y resistencia: Triunfo o fracas de la política indigenista?* Panamá: Editorial Mariano Arosemena.

———. 2015. "Panamá en la historia global." *Minervae Baeticae: Boletín de la Real Academia Sevillana de Buenas Letras* 43: 97–116. http://institucional.us.es/registers/rasbl/43/Alfredo Castillero Calvo.pdf.

CentralAmericaData. 2014. "Panama: More Revenue from Tourism than from Canal." April 7, 2014. https://www.centralamericadata.com/en/article/home/Panama_More_Revenue_From_Tourism_Than_From_Canal.

Chaney, Elsa, and Mary Garcia Castro. 1989. *Muchachas No More: Household Workers in Latin America and the Caribbean.* Philadelphia: Temple University.

Conniff, Michael. 1985. *Black Labor on a White Canal, 1904–1981.* Pittsburgh: University of Pittsburgh Press.

Cooke, Richard G. 1976. "El hombre y la tierra en el Panamá prehistórico." *Revista Nacional de Cultura* 2: 17–38.

———. 2005. "Prehistory of Native Americans on the Central American Land Bridge: Colonization, Dispersal and Divergence." *Journal of Archaeological Research* 13 (2): 129–87. https://doi.org/10.1007/s10804-005-2486-4.

———. 2015. "Orígenes, dispersión y supervivencia de las sociedades originarias de la sub-región istmeña de América: Una reseña en el marco de la historia profunda." In *Encuentro. El Mar del Sur: 500 años después. Una visión interdisciplinaria,* edited by Marcela Camargo, 25–53. Panamá: Editorial Universitaria Carlos Manuel Gasteazoro. Accessed August 19, 2019. https://aahpanama.org/wp-content/uploads/2016/04/Cooke-2016-Origenes-dispersion-y-supervivencia.pdf.

Cooke, Richard G., and Anthony J. Ranere. 1992a. "Human Influences on the Zoogeography of Panama: An Update Based on Archaeological and Ethnohistorical Evidence." In *Biogeography of Mesoamerica: Proceedings of a Symposium (Mérida, Yucatán, México, October 26–30, 1984),* edited by Steven P. Darwin and Arthur L. Welden, 21–58. Tulane: Mesoamerican Ecology Institute, Tulane University.

———. 1992b. "The Origin of Wealth and Hierarchy in the Central Region of Panama (12,000–2,000 BP), with Observations on its Relevance to the History and Phylogeny of Chibchan-Speaking Polities in Panama and Elsewhere." In *Wealth and Hierarchy in the Intermediate Area: A Symposium at Dumbarton Oaks, October 10 and 11,* edited by Frederick Lange, 243–316. Washington, DC: Dumbarton Oaks.

Cooke, Richard G., and Luis Alberto Sánchez Herrera. 2004. "Capítula I – Panamá Prehispánico." In *Historia general de Panamá: Las sociedades originarias* [volume 1, tome 2], edited by Alfredo Castillero Calvo, 3–89. Panamá: Comité Nacional del Centenario de la República.

Crappanzano, Vincent. 1980. *Tuhami: Portrait of a Moroccan.* Chicago: University of Chicago Press.

Credit Suisse. 2018. *Global Wealth Databook.* Zurich: Credit Suisse AG Research Institute. Accessed August 19, 2019. https://www.credit-suisse.com/media/assets/corporate/docs/about-us/research/publications/global-wealth-databook-2018.pdf.

Diaz, Jean Carlos. 2018. "Belisario Frías, uno de los corregimientos más 'calientes' de San Miguelito." *Díaadía*, February 4, 2018. https://www.diaadia.com.pa/el-pais/belisario-frias-uno-de-los-corregimientos-mas-calientes-de-san-miguelito-333110.

Edelman, Marc, Ruth Hall, Saturnino M. Borras Jr., Ian Scoones, Ben White, and Wendy Wolford, eds. 2018. *Global Land Grabbing and Political Reactions "From Below."* London: Routledge.

Ellis, Carolyn, Tony E. Adams, and Arthur P. Bochner. 2011. "Autoethnography: An Overview." *Historical Social Research* 36 (4): 273–90. https://www.jstor.org/stable/23032294.

Embassy of the Kingdom of the Netherlands in Panama. 2018. *Report: Agriculture in Panama – Challenges and Opportunities 2018*. The Hague: The Netherlands Ministry of Foreign Affairs. Accessed August 19, 2019. https://www.rvo.nl/sites/default/files/2018/03/agriculture-in-panama-challenges-and-opportunities-2018.pdf.

Fairbairn, Madeleine. 2020. *Fields of Gold: Financing the Global Land Rush.* Ithaca: Cornell University Press.

Farnsworth, David, and James McKenney. 1983. *U.S.-Panama Relations, 1903–1978: A Study in Linkage Politics.* Boulder, CO: Westview Press.

Figueroa Navarro, Alfredo. 1982. *Dominio y sociedad en el Panamá colombiano (1821–1903*). 3rd ed. Panamá: Editorial Universitaria.

Frank, Geyla. 1979. "Finding a Common Denominator: A Phenomenological Critique of Life History Method." *Ethos* 7, no. 1 (Spring): 68–94. https://doi.org/10.1525/eth.1979.7.1.02a00050.

———. 1995. "Anthropology and Individual Lives: The Story of the Life History and the History of the Life Story." *American Anthropologist* 97, no. 1 (March): 145–8.

Freire, Carolina. 2019. "La pobreza infantil." *La Prensa*, January 24, 2019. https://www.prensa.com/opinion/pobreza-infantil_0_5220977936.html.

Gandásegui, Marco Antonio, Jr. 1974. "La concentración del poder económico en Panamá." In *Panamá, dependencia y liberación*, edited by Ricaurte Soler, 99–183. San José, Costa Rica: Editorial Universitaria Centroamericana (EDUCA).

Gandásegui, Marco Antonio, Jr., and George Priestley. 1990. *Panama's Crisis: Is There a Democratic Alternative?* Working Paper No. 3. New York: City University of New York, Bildner Center for Western Hemisphere Studies.

Gascón, Jordi, and Diana Ojeda. 2014. *Turistas y campesinado: El turismo como vector de cambio de las economías campesinas en la era de la globalización.* Madrid, Spain: Foro de Turismo Responsable; Tenerife, Spain: Asociación Canaria de Antropología & PASOS, Revista de Turismo y Patrimonio Cultural. Accessed August 19, 2019. http://www.pasosonline.org/es/colecciones/pasos-edita/47-numero-12-turistas-y-campesinado-el-turismo-como-vector-de-cambio-de-las-economias-campesinas-en-la-era-de-la-globalizacion.

Gjording, Chris N. 1991. *Conditions Not of Their Choosing: The Guaymí Indians and Mining Multinationals in Panama*. Washington, DC: Smithsonian Institution Press.

Gmelch, Sharon. 1991. *Nan: The Life of an Irish Travelling Woman*. Prospect Heights, IL: Waveland Press.

Grandin, Greg. 2010. "It Was Heaven That They Burned." *The Nation*, September 8, 2010. https://www.thenation.com/article/archive/it-was-heaven-they-burned.

Guevara Mann, Carlos. 2011. "National Security or Special Interests? US Support for the Panama Canal Expansion Programme." *Global Society* 25 (2): 181–204. https://doi.org/10.1080/13600826.2011.553529.

Independent Commission of Inquiry on the U.S. Invasion of Panama. 1991. *The Truth Behind Operation "Just Cause."* Boston: South End Press.

Jaén Suárez, Omar. 1971. *El hombre y la tierra en Natá de 1700 a 1850*. Panamá: Editorial Universitaria.

———. 1978. *La población del Istmo de Panamá del siglo XVI al siglo XX*. Panamá: Impresora de La Nación. Translated from dissertation for University of Paris, Panteon-Sorbonne.

Joly, Luz Graciela. 1984. "La migración de los interioranos hacia la Costa Abajo." In *Colonización y destrucción de Bosques en Panamá*, edited by Stanley Heckadon Moreno and Alberto McKay, 63–80. Panama City, Panama: Asociación Panameña de Antropología.

Kahn, Carrie. 2016. "The $5 Billion Panama Canal Expansion Opens Sunday, Amidst Shipping Concerns." *NPR*, June 25, 2016. http://www.npr.org/2016/06/25/483523910/the-5-billion-panama-canal-expansion-opens-sunday-amidst-shipping-concerns.

Koster, R. M., and Guillermo Sánchez. 1990. *In the Time of Tyrants – Panama: 1968–1990*. New York: W.W. Norton.

Kovaleski, Serge F. 1999. "In a Ceremony, U.S. Turns Over Panama Canal." *Washington Post* [Foreign Service Archives], December 15, 1999, A01. Accessed August 19, 2019. http://www.washingtonpost.com/wp-srv/WPcap/1999-12/15/097r-121599-idx.html.

LaFeber, Walter. 1979. *The Panama Canal: The Crisis in Historical Perspective*. New York: Oxford University Press.

Lardieri, Alexa. 2018. "World Bank: Half the World Lives on Less than $5.50 a Day." *U.S. News*, October 17, 2018. Accessed August 19, 2019. http://www.usnews.com/news/economy/articles/2018-10-17/world-bank-half-the-world-lives-on-less-than-550-a-day.

Lasso, Marixa. 2019. *Erased*. Cambridge, MA: Harvard University Press.

Lasso, Mileika. 2016. "Pobreza en Panamá alcanza al 50% de la población rural." *La Estrella de Panamá*, December 27, 2016. https://www.laestrella.com.pa/economia/161227/50-panama-pobreza-alcanza.

Leis, Raúl. 1999. "Nunca, nunca más …" *El Panamá América*, December 15, 1999, A10. https://www.panamaamerica.com.pa/opinion/nunca-nunca-mas-73777/amp.

Lewis, Oscar. 1961. *The Children of Sanchez: Autobiography of a Mexican Family*. New York: Random House.

———. 1966. *La Vida: A Puerto Rican Family in the Culture of Poverty*. New York: Random House.

Lurie, Nancy Oestreich, ed. 1961. *Mountain Wolf Woman, Sister of Crashing Thunder: The Autobiography of a Winnebago Woman*. Ann Arbor: University of Michigan Press.

Manduley, Julio. 1980. "Panama: Dependent Capitalism and Beyond – The Linkage with World Economy Through the Sphere of Circulation." *Latin American Perspectives* 7 (2–3): 57–74. https://doi.org/10.1177%2F0094582X8000700205.

McWatters, Mason. 2009. *Residential Tourism: (De)Constructing Paradise*. Tonawanda, NY: Channel View Publications.

Mellado, María Eugenia. 2011. "Implantar turismo: ?sembrar desarrollo? El caso del archipiélago de Las Perlas, Panamá." Master's thesis, Universidad de Lleida, Facultad de Letras.

Mintz, Sidney W. 1974. *Worker in the Cane: A Puerto Rican Life History*. New York: W.W. Norton. First published 1960.

Mufson, Steven. 2016. "An Expanded Panama Canal Opens for Giant Ships." *Washington Post*. June 26, 2016. https://www.washingtonpost.com/world/the_americas/an-expanded-panama-canal-opens-for-giant-ships/2016/06/26/11a93574-37d1-11e6-af02-1df55f0c77ff_story.html.

Müller-Schwarze, Nina K. 2015. *The Blood of Victoriano Lorenzo: An Ethnography of the Cholos of Northern Coclé Province, Panama*. Jefferson, NC: McFarland & Company, Inc.

Nash, June. 1992. *I Spent My Life in the Mines: The Story of Juan Rojas, Bolivian Tin Miner*. New York: Columbia University Press.

Nazario, Jesus, and Jess Cherofsky. 2020. "'The Communities Know We Are Managing the Forest Well': Rainforest and Sacred Site in Guatemala at Risk of Privatization by U.S. Archaeologist." *Cultural Survival*, July 24, 2020. Accessed August 18, 2020. https://www.culturalsurvival.org/news/communities-know-we-are-managing-forest-well-rainforest-and-sacred-site-guatemala-risk.

*New York Times*. 2012. "The 45 Places to Go in 2012." *New York Times* [Travel Section]. January 6, 2012. https://www.nytimes.com/2012/01/08/travel/45-places-to-go-in-2012.html.

———. 2019. "52 Places to Go in 2019." *New York Times* [Travel Section]. Last updated January 18, 2019. https://www.nytimes.com/interactive/2019/travel/places-to-visit.html.

O'Dea, Aaron, Harilaos A. Lessios, Anthony G. Coates, Ron I. Eytan, Sergio A. Restrepo-Moreno, Alberto L. Cione, Laurel S. Collins, and Alan de Queiroz. 2016. "Formation of the Isthmus of Panama." *Science Advances* 2 (8). https://doi.org/10.1126/sciadv.1600883.

Okely, Judith 1992. "Anthropology and Autobiography: Participatory Experience and Embodied Knowledge." In *Anthropology and Autobiography*, ASA Monographs No. 29, edited by Judith Okely and Helen Callaway, 1–28. London: Routledge.

Opazo Bernales, Andrés. 1988. *Panamá: La iglesia y la lucha de los pobres*. San Jose, Costa Rica: Editorial DEI.

Perego, Ugo A., Hovirag Lancioni, Maribel Tribaldos, Norman Angerhofer, Jayne E. Ekins, Anna Olivieri, Scott R. Woodward, Juan Miguel Pascale, Richard Cooke, Jorge Motta, and Alessandro Achilli. 2012. "Decrypting the Mitochondrial Gene Pool of Modern Panamanians." *PLoS* ONE 7 (6): e38337. https://doi.org/10.1371/journal.pone.0038337.

Preston, R.J., and M.-A. Tremblay. 2006. "Anthropology in Canada." In *The Canadian Encyclopedia*. Last modified January 17, 2017. https://www.thecanadianencyclopedia.ca/en/article/anthropology.

Priestley, George. 1986. *Military Government and Popular Participation in Panama: The Torrijos Regime, 1968–1975*. Boulder, CO: Westview Press.

Radin, Paul. 1926. *The Autobiography of a Winnebago Indian*. New York: Appleton and Co.

Ranere, Anthony J. 2006. "The Clovis Colonization of Central America." In *Paleoindian Archaeology: A Hemispheric Perspective*, edited by Juliet E. Morrow and Cristóbal Gnecco, 69–85. Gainesville: University of Florida Press.

Reed-Danahay, Deborah E., ed. 1997. *Auto/Ethnography: Rewriting the Self and the Social*. Oxford: Berg.

Ricord, Humberto E. 1991. *Noriega y Panamá: Orgía y aplastamiento de la narcodictadura*. Mexico, DF: Impr. Eficiencia.

Robinson, William I. 2012. "Latin America in the New Global Capitalism." *NACLA Report on the Americas* 45 (2): 13–18. https://doi.org/10.1080/10714839.2012.11722083.

Rodríquez Blanco, Eugenia, with Francisco Herrera. Forthcoming. *Mujeres Indígenas Migrantes: Encrucijadas de género y etnicidad en la migración indígena contemporánea en Panamá*. Quito, Ecuador: Editorial Abya Yala.

Rosas Quirós, Gaspar. 1972. Primer centenario de la provincia de Coclé, 1855–1955. Programa Conmemorativo del 12 de Septiembre de 1955. http://bdigital.binal.ac.pa/bdp/primer centenario1.pdf.

Rubbo, Anna, and Michael Taussig. 1978. "Up Off Their Knees: Servanthood in Southwest Colombia." In *Female Servants and Economic Development*, University of Michigan Occasional Papers in Women's Studies No. 1, edited by Louise Tilly, 5–29. Ann Arbor: University of Michigan.

Rudolf, Gloria. 1983. "Panamanian Insights into a Common Third World Trio: Capitalism, Labor Migration and Class Conflict." In *Panama in Transition: Local Reactions to Development Policies*, University of Missouri Monographs in Anthropology No. 6., edited by John Bort and Mary Helms, 129–60. Columbia, MO: University of Missouri Monographs in Anthropology.

———. 1992. "When Servants Could Always Go Home." *Cultural Survival Quarterly* 16: 28–30.

———. 1999. *Panama's Poor – Victims, Agents, and Historymakers*. Gainesville: University Press of Florida.

———. 2000. *La gente pobre de Panamá – Víctimas, agentes, y hacedores de la historia*. Panamá: Editorial Universitaria.

———. 2003. "Migraciones rurales-urbanas en Panamá: Vínculos socioeconómicos y el factor de género." *Mesoamérica* 24 (45): 131–47.

———. 2014. "Desarrollo, ¿Para quién y hasta cuándo?. Impactos del turismo residencial en zonas rurales de Panamá." *Canto Rodado* 9: 85–110.

Rudolf Frazier, Gloria. 1976. "Moving to Stand Still: Third World Poverty and Rural-to-Urban Migration – A Panamanian Case History." PhD diss., University of Pittsburgh, Department of Anthropology.

Scranton, Margaret E. 1991. *The Noriega Years*. Boulder, CO: Lynne Rienner Publishers.

Sharma, Gaurav. 2018. "Expanded Panama Canal Feels Benign Impact of U.S. Oil and Gas Exports to Asia." *Forbes*, April 16, 2018. Accessed August 20, 2019. http://www.forbes.com/sites/gauravsharma/2018/04/16/expanded-panama-canal-feels-benign-impact-of-u-s-oil-and-gas-exports-to-asia/#62a6e8307b02.

Shostak, Marjorie. 1981. *Nisa: The Life and Words of a !Kung Woman*. New York: Vintage.

Smith, Margo. 1973. "Domestic Service as a Channel of Upward Mobility for the Lower Class Woman: The Lima Case." In *Female and Male in Latin America*, edited by Ann Pescatello, 191–207. Pittsburgh: University of Pittsburgh Press.

Spalding, Ana K. 2013. "Lifestyle Migration to Bocas del Toro, Panama: Exploring Migration Strategies and Introducing Local Implications of the Search for Paradise. *International Review of Social Research* 3 (1): 65–84.

Theodossopoulos, Dimitrios. 2015. "Sharing Anthropological Knowledge, Decolonizing Anthropology: Emberá Indigeneity and Engaged Anthropology." In *Indigenous Studies and Engaged Anthropology: The Collaborative Moment*, edited by Paul Sillitoe, 33–54. Burlington, VT: Ashgate Publishing Company.

Underhill, Ruth. 1961. "Forward." In *Mountain Wolf Woman, Sister of Crashing Thunder: The Autobiography of a Winnebago Woman*, edited by Nancy Oestreich Lurie, vii–ix. Ann Arbor: University of Michigan Press.

UNICEF. 2017. *UNICEF Annual Report 2017: Panama*. New York: UNICEF. Accessed August 20, 2019. http://www.unicef.org/about/annualreport/files/Panama_2017_COAR.pdf.

Vega Loo, Manuel. 2019. "Producto interno bruto de Panamá creció 3.7% durante 2018." *La Prensa*, March 1, 2019. Accessed August 20, 2019. http://www.prensa.com/economia/Producto-interno-bruto-Panama-crecio_0_5248725091.html.

Velasquez Runk, Julie. 2014. "Enriching Indigenous Knowledge Scholarship via Collaborative Methodologies: Beyond the High Tide's Few Hours." *Ecology and Society* 19 (4): 37.

Waterston, Alisse. 2005. "The Story of My Story: An Anthropology of Violence, Dispossession, and Diaspora." *Anthropological Quarterly* 78 (1): 43–61. https://doi.org/10.1353/anq.2005.0018.

———. 2019. "Intimate Ethnography and the Anthropological Imagination: Dialectical Aspects of the Personal and Political in *My Father's Wars. American Ethnologist* 46 (1): 7–19. https://doi.org/10.1111/amet.12730.

Weil, Thomas E., Jan Knippers Black, Howard I. Blutstein, David S. McMorris, Frederick P. Munson, and Charles Townsend. 1972. *Area Handbook for Panama*. Washington, DC: Foreign Area Studies, The American University.

Wikipedia. 2011. "Vasco Núñez de Balboa: Early Career." Accessed August 20, 2019. http://en.wikipedia.org/wiki/Vasco_Núñez_de_Balboa#Early_career.

———. 2020. "COVID-19 Pandemic Death Rates by Country." Updated November 30, 2020. Accessed December 3, 2020. https://en.wikipedia.org/wiki/COVID-19_pandemic_death_rates_by_country.

Wolf, Margery. 1992. *A Thrice Told Tale: Feminism, Postmodernism, and Ethnographic Responsibility*. Stanford: Stanford University Press.

World Bank. 1999. *Panama-Poverty Assessment: Priorities and Strategies for Poverty Reduction*. Washington, DC: Latin America and the Caribbean Region Human Development Department. June 28, 1999. Accessed August 20, 2019. http://documents.worldbank.org/curated/en/142081468774918874/pdf/multi-page.pdf.

———. 2018. "The World Bank in Panama, Overview." Where We Work / Panama [World Bank website]. Updated April, 2019. Accessed August 20, 2019. http://www.worldbank.org/en/country/panama/overview.

———. 2020. "The World Bank in Panama, Overview." Where We Work / Panama [World Bank website]. Updated October 2020. Accessed November 24, 2020. http://www.worldbank.org/en/country/panama/overview.

Zimbalist, Andrew, and John Weeks. 1991. *Panama at the Crossroads: Economic Development and Political Change in the Twentieth Century*. Berkeley: University of California Press.

Zindar, John M. 1988. "Opposition Outflanked." *NACLA Report on the Americas* 22 (4): 31–8. https://doi.org/10.1080/10714839.1988.11723305.

# Index

# TC TEACHING CULTURE

## Ethnographies for the Classroom

Editor: John Barker, University of British Columbia

This series is an essential resource for instructors searching for ethnographic case studies that are contemporary, engaging, provocative, and created specifically with undergraduate students in mind. Written with clarity and personal warmth, books in the series introduce students to the core methods and orienting frameworks of ethnographic research and provide a compelling entry point to some of the most urgent issues faced by people around the globe today.

### Recent Books in the Series

*Esperanza Speaks: Confronting a Century of Global Change in Rural Panama* by Gloria Rudolf (2021)
*The Living Inca Town: Tourist Encounters in the Peruvian Andes* by Karoline Guelke (2021)
*Collective Care: Indigenous Motherhood, Family, and HIV/AIDS* by Pamela J. Downe (2021)
*I Was Never Alone, or Oporniki: An Ethnographic Play on Disability in Russia* by Cassandra Hartblay (2020)
*Millennial Movements: Positive Social Change in Urban Costa Rica* by Karen Stocker (2020)
*From Water to Wine: Becoming Middle Class in Angola* by Jess Auerbach (2020)
*Deeply Rooted in the Present: Heritage, Memory, and Identity in Brazilian Quilombos* by Mary Lorena Kenny (2018)
*Long Night at the Vepsian Museum: The Forest Folk of Northern Russia and the Struggle for Cultural Survival* by Veronica Davidov (2017)
*Truth and Indignation: Canada's Truth and Reconciliation Commission on Indian Residential Schools*, second edition, by Ronald Niezen (2017)
*Merchants in the City of Art: Work, Identity, and Change in a Florentine Neighborhood* by Anne Schiller (2016)
*Ancestral Lines: The Maisin of Papua New Guinea and the Fate of the Rainforest*, second edition, by John Barker (2016)
*Love Stories: Language, Private Love, and Public Romance in Georgia* by Paul Manning (2015)
*Culturing Bioscience: A Case Study in the Anthropology of Science* by Udo Krautwurst (2014)

*Fields of Play: An Ethnography of Children's Sports* by Noel Dyck (2012)
*Made in Madagascar: Sapphires, Ecotourism, and the Global Bazaar* by Andrew Walsh (2012)
*Red Flags and Lace Coiffes: Identity and Survival in a Breton Village* by Charles R. Menzies (2011)
*Rites of the Republic: Citizens' Theatre and the Politics of Culture in Southern France* by Mark Ingram (2011)

www.ingramcontent.com/pod-product-compliance
Lightning Source LLC
LaVergne TN
LVHW010347080826
844660LV00003B/215
*9781487594701*